HIS FATHER SAW HIM COMING

HIS FATHER SAW HIM COMING

· · · · · · · · · · ·

JIM KRAUS

Tyndale House Publishers, Inc.
WHEATON, ILLINOIS

Library of Congress Cataloging-in-Publication Data

Krause, Jim.
    His father saw him coming / Jim Kraus.
        p.   cm.
    ISBN 0-8423-6588-5
    1. Christian life—1960-   2. God—Love.   3. Love—Religious
aspects—Christianity.   4. Kraus, Jim.   I. Title.
BV4501.2.K69   1994
242—dc20   94-12491

Printed in the United States of America

00 99 98 97 96 95
8   7   6   5   4   3   2

To my father,
who told me his stories,
and to my wife, Terri,
who listens to mine

Contents

Acknowledgments

I would like to thank the people of the Glen Ellyn Bible Church, who first heard some of my stories at our Common Ground outreach services. Their affirmation and encouragement was greatly appreciated. I would also like to thank Pastor Gary Gulbranson, who asked me to participate. Special thanks also go to the whole Common Ground team for their enthusiasm and friendship: Perry Mascetti, Wes Wetherell, Mike Salvatori, Don Baddorf, Lisa Gaylord, Pastor Jeff Helton, Jim Swanson, and LuAnne Zaeske.

Many thanks also to Wightman Weese, my editor at Tyndale House, who helped polish these stories, initially written to be told aloud, into stories ready to come alive from the written word.

One

The Inheritance

Praise the Lord. Blessed is the man who fears the Lord, who finds great delight in his commands. His children will be mighty in the land; the generation of the upright will be blessed. Wealth and riches are in his house, and his righteousness endures forever. Even in darkness light dawns for the upright, for the gracious and compassionate and righteous man. Good will come to him who is generous and lends freely, who conducts his affairs with justice. Surely he will never be shaken; a righteous man will be remembered forever. (Psalm 112:1-6)

On my desk I have a stained and tattered gray ledger, worn threadbare at the corners. It is my father's last ledger used at the last bakery that he owned. When he retired, he tore out the pages showing the numbers of bags of flour on order and the store's cash-register tallies.

With a number two pencil, he began to write about the past. His autobiography began in 1882 with stories he had learned at his father's knee.

My father went to school only until the eighth grade—not a well-educated man. He could read and write, and he knew his arithmetic. In his eighth-grade script, he wrote more than two hundred pages of our family history spanning more than a hundred years.

My grandfather often said that to be a complete scholar, one needed to know geography. And this is what I know of my grandfather's geography.

If you look back through the fog of history, you might see my great-great-great-great-grandfather, who was born in southern Germany several hundred years ago. He migrated with his family to Romania, to a spot along the southern border of what was then called Transylvania. He was seeking stability and land with a future, a place to call home, a place to belong.

My great-grandfather was a blacksmith, who could do most anything with a forge and anvil. Most of his day was spent repairing farm wagons, fixing the metal rims that encircled the wagon wheels, mending hitches and axles. Heating the wagon parts in the forge until they glowed a dull orange, he would pound out the defects on a massive anvil.

Peter Martin Kraus, my grandfather, was born in 1882 in the small village of Woltz. Woltz is not now, nor was then, much of a village. A scattering of small dusty buildings, a small school building, and a tiny Lutheran church, Woltz was connected to the outside world by a rutted and muddy one-wagon track. Behind virtually every home was a small plot of vegetables—rows of cabbage, potatoes, and flax. The poor peasants often raised chickens, goats, pigs, and oxen.

My grandfather Peter did not have a carefree childhood. In 1894, the twelve-year-old boy was forced into an apprenticeship to a local baker in Kopisch, a small village a few miles south. Times were hard, and except for those who were lucky and born into a privileged family, children entered the working life at a very early age.

His family was neither lucky nor privileged.

To be an apprentice was almost like being adopted. My grandfather was "given" to the local baker for a three-year period. He slept on a straw-filled mattress in a small alcove above the stable. The baker's wife prepared his food. He complained that the food they gave their pigs was better than what he received.

The days were long and tedious. Peter had to rise at 2 A.M. to fire the brick oven. The bakery lacked even the simplest of machinery. Ingredients for the heavy rye breads had to be measured into waist-high wooden troughs and laboriously mixed by hand. The dark bakery was lit with only a coal-oil lantern and a few candles. Young Peter, often exhausted by the work, would sleep on the sacks of flour, too tired to walk up to his room. Beside the long hours and the hot, back-breaking work, Peter endured frequent verbal and physical beatings at the hand of the owner.

After one too many beatings with the baker's wide leather strap, young Peter had had enough. He knew he deserved better treatment. He picked up his few meager belongings, took a loaf of bread, and ran. But in a small town, how far can a thirteen-year-old run?

He hid out under a nearby wooden bridge for three days. He could hear the local police as they searched for him, their heels echoing on the wooden planks inches above his hiding place. It was illegal for anyone to escape their apprenticeship, and Peter faced two years in the local jail, where conditions would be much worse.

In the middle of the third night, cold, wet, and hungry, he silently crept to his parents' tiny two-room house. His mother held him and comforted him. After a hot meal, Peter faced his future with courage and marched to the police station to turn himself in.

Accusations and threats followed, and the baker eventually agreed to take him back, promising no reprisals. Later, Peter would recall that working and living conditions improved after his return—but only a little.

The baker took Peter back because he was a talented baker and hard worker. When other apprentices delivered the rye bread and rolls to local shops and houses, they could only carry one basket at a time. Peter would carry two and sometimes three.

At the age of sixteen, he was a qualified journey-man baker. He could bake everything from rich, dense rye breads to sweet, delicate cookies.

Romania of 1898 was a poor, very isolated, back-water country. Jobs were scarce, and what few jobs there were paid little for long hours of hard work. The town of Woltz was a very long way from the glittering cultural capitals of Europe.

At sixteen years of age, Peter knew there was more to life than this. If he stayed in Woltz, he would be no more than a poorly paid baker. Young Peter heard from friends who had gone out in search of work that the coal mines in Germany were begging for workers with strong backs and arms to mine coal.

It was a dirty and life-threatening job, chiseling coal from the ground, inhaling mouthfuls of coal dust and soot. But it paid twice the wages of a skilled baker. Peter knew his family could use the extra money.

In the summer of 1898, Peter hugged his mother, shook hands with his father, and set out for Germany. There was no stagecoach to board or train that Peter could afford. He had no legal travel documents, no passport.

There was only one choice: He walked.

It was to be a journey of at least eight hundred miles, about the distance from Chicago to New York City. As he started west that day, he turned often to see his parents and his home fade into the eastern horizon. He walked west into Hungary and on to Budapest. From there, he walked northwest, crossing the Carpathian Mountains and into Czechoslovakia.

He walked to Prague and into the southern part of Germany and west to the coal fields near the Rhine River.

It took Peter nearly a month to make the eight-hundred-mile trip. He skirted the main border crossings since he had no legal travel documents. He climbed off the mountain roads in the Carpathians and made his way through dark and dangerous passes at night. He slept under the stars in the clear weather. In the rain, he sought out old barns or dense woods. He traded a day's work for a hot meal where he could. He ate green apples found in the woods along the way.

At sixteen, he worked sixty hours a week with a pickax and shovel in the dark mine shafts and sent most of his wages back home.

Peter returned home to Romania at the turn of the century to serve in the Romanian army, required of all able-bodied men. Badly injured during basic training, he was discharged to recuperate. In less than three months, hard times forced him to return to the coal mines. Again he walked the eight hundred miles. This time he spent five years in the coal shafts. His wages enabled his parents to buy a few acres of land that bordered a small creek.

Peter was now twenty-three and seeking a better life. He yearned for freedom and a future. American factory agents spread news of unlimited opportunity across the ocean. Peter realized that his future was farther west. With his friend John Loew, Peter said good-bye once again to family and friends . . . and set off for America.

My grandfather told the story of his first train ride—from New York to Pittsburgh. The train stopped at a small town in the Allegheny Mountains. Peter and John pulled out a few pennies from their pockets and bought what looked like strange yellow cucumbers from a peddler at the station. They ate them, skins and all, never before having seen bananas.

The two friends arrived in Homestead, just east of Pittsburgh, where several others from their hometown had settled. "I was alone in this country," my grandfather said. "But I was free."

This is only part of Peter's story. There is much more, of course. Of the stories left untold, you would hear how my father came to be born and how they came to move back to Romania for a time, and many other wonderful things.

You may wonder how I know so much about my grandfather. You may have thought I spent hours at his knee as he told me these wonderful tales and family history.

I tell people I knew my grandfather well, though I never actually met him. He died a year before I entered the world, so he never saw me and I never heard his voice. He never had the chance to tell his stories directly to me. Instead it comes in my father's story, written in pencil, in simple, eighth-grade-level script.

It isn't a story about genetics or inherited characteristics or about my grandfather's blond hair and blue eyes. It is about character. That old ledger is perhaps the greatest gift my father could have given his

7

children. It is the story of a victorious past for me to read as I face the future.

My father ended his story:

> This takes me to 1960 where each one of our children will be able to carve their own histories and continue from where I left off, each one to his or her own memory of what I have related in these past pages. I have mentioned only a small amount of the activities that I encountered, leaving your imagination to roam.
>
> I've been thrilled with each day, rising early, to see what that day had in store for me, calling on the Lord to give me strength and guidance to carry me forward and also asking for forgiveness for the times that I may have gone astray.
>
> Wishing you all good histories in the time ever present, I remain as ever, an admiring father.

It is a story about a life and how it was lived. It is about courage. It is about being unafraid. My grandfather, a brave, strong, daring, and faithful man, leaves in my father's journal stories that have defined the person I am today. My grandfather, walking eight hundred miles to work in the coal mines to support his family, leaves me the challenge that I should be able to endure most anything, following the example he left for me.

It is much the same in the Christian life. We have

in the Bible the same kind of family stories of daring and bravery and compassion. Because of my grandfather's courage, I have known what courage is. I have tried to be courageous as well. The way I live my life I hope will also be a tribute to my father, who told and retold those stories of bravery and sacrifice to us when we were children. So, this is where I take up—not with a lead pencil on the back pages of a used ledger but using a somewhat more sophisticated way of writing—to tell the next chapter in the Kraus story my great-grandfather started years ago.

Two

The Narrow Road

Do not deceive yourselves. If any one of you
thinks he is wise by the standards of this age, he
should become a "fool" so that he may become
wise. For the wisdom of this world is foolishness
in God's sight. As it is written: "He catches the
wise in their craftiness"; and again, "The Lord
knows that the thoughts of the wise are futile." So
then, no more boasting about men! All things are
yours, whether Paul or Apollos or Cephas or the
world or life or death or the present or the future—
all are yours, and you are of Christ, and Christ is
of God. (1 Corinthians 3:18-23)

John F. Kennedy is president; the Beatles have yet
to be discovered; the world is a wonderful place.
The year is 1962. I am twelve years old and on the
border between the child and adult worlds. My teen
years are shimmering in front of me, just months
away. It is the fall of the year, and there is a dry,
rustling coolness in the air.

I grew up in western Pennsylvania on the far edge
of a small town called Jeannette. Our claim to fame
was that we were the only town in America called
Jeannette. It's a good place to be from.

One exception to my wonderful life was that from
9 to 11 A.M. every Saturday morning between September and June, 1962, I was trapped in the basement of
our church. The sturdy, Gothic structure, built of sandstone and red brick, sat at the top of Clay Avenue,
overlooking the railroad tracks and the abandoned
passenger station. Our denomination required a yearlong catechism class for the entire youth group in
order for us to be confirmed as members.

And what I learned one Saturday morning would
have a profound impact on the next eighteen years of
my life.

In class, I sat between Bob Stough, who eventually
would become a recluse—an actual hermit—and
Rod Heasley, who we called Pez because he had a
couple of full Pez dispensers in his pockets at all
times. The class had to memorize the Lord's Prayer,
the Ten Commandments, the Apostles' Creed—along
with other tenets of the faith—in order to graduate
into adulthood.

We would recite them in a breathless torrent of

words, afraid that if we stopped to inhale, the words would stop as well. We could not let our tongues relax; we would not allow our minds to pause, for the words were held in our short-term memories with a white-knuckle grip.

Every Friday night my mother would remind me and remind me and remind me that I had to finish my catechism lesson for the following morning. On a regular basis, I would have a spoonful of cornflakes in one hand and a pencil in the other, trying desperately to complete the lesson by 8:50 A.M., the last possible minute I could wait until I had to get on my bike and pedal furiously to the church.

For six months of catechism lessons, our lay pastor taught the group. We considered him the "second string" of the pastoral staff. He was a part-time pastor and a full-time high school civics teacher who seldom smiled and adopted a serious, almost medieval look. He appeared to enjoy himself as he flowed through the Sunday services in his long black robe with a dour ecclesiastical frown on his face.

In our church, the ministers wore robes and collars and purple vestments. When they read from the Bible, they finished each passage with the somber incantation of "Thus endeth the Scripture for this day."

Ominous and distant, these men were. Robed in black and speaking in words and terms that no twelve-year-old I knew understood, they were the very guardians of heaven. Theology must flow from them.

On this particular Saturday, the basement room in the church was filled with twelve-year-olds, anxious to be anywhere other than the church basement. Our behavior fluctuated between squirmy and giggly and aggressive and obnoxious.

The lay pastor stood before us. He was wearing street clothes—a coat and tie—and the difference was disconcerting and troubling. We assumed that he always wore a robe.

He was retelling the story of the camel and the eye of the needle. He explained the Needle was an actual gate in the wall of the city of Jerusalem. It was not a literal needle and thread. This was truly enlightening. Until that moment, I had taken it literally and the illustration made absolutely no sense at all.

He stopped. Scowling at us and speaking very slowly, in darker and deeper tones, his words still reverberate in my memory: "The path to heaven is very, very narrow. That is what this story about the rich man and the camel teaches us."

And then, looking straight at me, he added, "And very, very few of you will make it to heaven. Very, very few of you are that good or that well behaved."

That was true, up to a point . . .

. . . and, of course, all good Christians would have immediately added, "But you all can go to heaven if you just accept Jesus as your Savior."

His words echoed throughout the basement. "None of you are that well behaved."

There was no next line. He glared at us, hoping he had scared us into obedience, which he had. After a few moments, he went on to whatever it was we had to memorize for that week.

This poor man is not to blame for this error in

theology, this twist in scriptural interpretation. He was sincere and no doubt meant well.

But there was one twelve-year-old who said to himself that day, "I know I can never be that good. If only a few of us are going to make it to heaven, and if I try to be good all my life and I don't make it into heaven, why, I'll have missed out on a lot of fun. So why bother trying?"

There is no blame to be assigned for anyone bumping me off the road to glory. I wanted an excuse; an excuse to not be good, and this was the best excuse I could imagine. The pastor was the catalyst, but I carried and nurtured all the right chemicals.

And for the next eighteen years of my life, the idea of an eternal reward or punishment or heaven and hell meant absolutely nothing to me. I was out to have a good time. And I did.

Didn't my family care? Wasn't there someone who had seen this sort of thing happen and would have turned me back onto the road, pointed in the right direction?

The simple answer is that there was not. My family is made up of wonderful people, but this part of basic theology was beyond them at the time. "Being saved" was not part of our vocabulary. And I was a relatively good person. I stayed out of jail, got good grades in school, obeyed most of my parents' wishes. Simply put, our dinner table conversation never included our soul's relationship with our Creator.

What about other Christians?

I have searched through my memories of those

eighteen years, and with all honesty I can say that
I never knowingly met or had a serious encounter
with any born-again Christian. I ran into a few street-
corner preachers, a few people passing out tracts, a
few Jehovah's Witnesses. But no close friend, no
casual acquaintance ever tried to call me back to God.

Funny, isn't it, how little effort it took to bump me
off the path to God. How many others were bumped
at the same time? But this is one of the ways in
which Satan works.

From that point until 1979, I had stopped worrying about the fate of my eternal soul. I was more
concerned about more temporal things—things like
parties, pleasures, and fun.

The pastor's words echoed in my memory—there
was no hope for a sinner like me. Why keep on trying to be good? But there was a small voice, a distant
light, a faint echo that kept part of me attuned to
matters of the spirit.

Through a chain of events, some wonderful Christians entered my life (one of whom later became
my wife). There was, however, one person in particular who went over to the jukebox, kicked it, and
stopped the record from skipping over and over and
over in the very same spot.

For the previous seventeen years, I had been master of my life, controlling my own destiny.

"Home" at this time was Chattanooga, Tennessee.
Work had brought me south. Two friends from work
were marrying. At their wedding, I enjoyed their
pastor's style and sense of humor. He was young and
dynamic. That day, a rite of passage had occurred—

the pastor and I were the same age. Until then, pastors were old guys with knobby dispositions and archaic theological attitudes.

I was intrigued—intrigued enough to attend his church the following weekend. Not only was he funny, he spoke in a language that I understood. He made sense. One Sunday later, on the church's visitor registration pad, I checked the box "wants to talk to a pastor." Those "eternal life" questions nagged at the inside of me. I wanted to put them into perspective—with a pastor's help. I didn't want to believe. I didn't want to give up my role of master of my universe. I just wanted the questions defused. I just wanted to stop worrying.

My phone rang; the pastor was on the line and said, "Let's do lunch." He named a restaurant that was famous for burgers, barbecue, loud music, and wild Saturday nights. I agreed and hung up—then thought a minute. Wait a second. Preachers don't go to places like that. They go to Howard Johnson.

We had a great lunch. (The music was softer during lunch.) And we had an illuminating discussion. At our second lunch, he asked if I would like to bless the meal. Unexpectedly, I choked up, throat closed, and I hoarsely croaked that I didn't know the right words.

He looked over at me, smiled, and bowed his head. He prayed for the food, and he prayed that the Lord would grant this poor fighter—me—the strength to put down his arms and give up the fight.

I didn't come to know Christ that day, but it wasn't much later until I did. That was the first time

I saw Christ out of the church, the first time that the message of God met me where I was, the first time I realized that the message of the Bible was meant for normal people who may not be in church on Sunday.

My pastor friend in Chattanooga did not make a practice of witnessing in bars. But he knew a person like me had built up strong antichurch defenses. In a bar, where I felt comfortable, those weapons were useless. It took a lot of courage for this man to step out of the role of a "pastor in the church" to that of a friend. If he hadn't, odds are I would still be lost.

He visited the sick in the hospital. He didn't wait until I was well to witness to me. He allowed me to realize that I was fighting with God, using my wits and will. He allowed me to realize the desperation of that fight. When I was off that road to glory, it was indeed a jungle of enticements and pleasures and evil. And I was battling the injustice and falsities and perversity and all the world's evil with my own intellect. It was hard, lonely work.

This pastor realized the situation. He put his arm around my shoulder and said it was OK to have questions and doubts and fears, but that I must know that there is indeed only one road, only one road to peace and eternal life.

I discovered that the road to God has no steep curbs or unclimbable guardrails—nothing that could prevent a sinner like me from getting back on the road. The outstretched hand of a friend, his willingness to meet me where I was, was all it took for this sinner to turn around.

Three

The Flood

*God is our refuge and strength, an ever-present
help in trouble. Therefore we will not fear, though
the earth give way and the mountains fall into the
heart of the sea, though its waters roar and foam
and the mountains quake with their surging.
(Psalm 46:1-3)*

When I was young, my hometown of Jeannette was
alive and vibrant and a great place to be a kid. A
quick two-mile bike ride and I would be downtown.
I spent hours at the G. C. Murphy Five & Dime
store reading every comic book displayed on the wire

racks by the stairway. At least until I was chased out by the lady with the black rhinestone glasses and hairnet.

"This isn't a library, you know."

I heard that line hundreds of times, and even today I look over my shoulder when I scan a magazine at a newsstand. I nervously wait . . . to hear that voice again.

And afterwards I would get a Black Cow—root beer and ice cream—for a quarter at Daugherty's Drugstore.

Two miles and back home again, I would cruise past the Oakford Park swimming pool and picnic grounds. Oakford Park was the site of the terrifying flood of 1894. The waters of Brush Creek, up until that hot summer day, gently meandered through the park. That afternoon, the stream, its waters churning from an afternoon thunderstorm, cascaded over the narrow banks and roared through the picnic grounds, sweeping a dozen people to their watery fate.

But as a child, being lost or swept away like that were just words in a book to me. My summers were bright and warm and happy.

We lived on the outskirts of town, where our home stood on a half-dozen acres of trees, black-berry bushes, and fields. The boundary of the north side of our property was that slow-flowing Brush Creek, a great place to fish, play pirates . . . be a kid.

It was a few weeks before Easter of 1959. Besides chocolate rabbits and jelly beans, Easter meant one very important thing to this nine-year-old. It meant

new pets. Two or three weeks before Easter, the
G. C. Murphy store in Jeannette would begin to sell
live baby chicks.

I would walk down the green linoleum–covered
stairs at Murphy's and head straight to my favorite
seasonal display. At the one end of an aisle, a four-by-
four-foot section of the counter would be left open,
with six-inch-high glass walls and a straw matting on
the floor. In the pen were hundreds of baby chicks
peeping and chirping and flapping their wings. Two
or three bare light bulbs suspended close to the
chicks provided warmth. In the corner were two
upturned mason jars with metal metering gadgets
screwed on to the threads. One jar contained chicken
feed and the other water.

Often, the chick's wispy down was dyed bright
pastel Easter colors—pinks and greens and laven-
ders—to be sold as living Easter pets.

My parents were only one generation removed
from the farms of the old country, so raising chickens was normal. My grandparents lived in a soot-
covered row house in Pittsburgh and yet always
kept a few chickens in a backyard pen to be fat-
tened for Sunday dinners.

I could buy two Easter chicks, along with all the
necessary food and supplies, for no more than a
dollar or two. And so I always bought chickens,
which we would raise in a pen in the backyard. And
then come summer, we would have a chicken dinner.

I never much cared about the grown-up chickens.
A full-grown chicken is not a pet. A farmer in
Minnesota once told me that a chicken wakes up

in a new world every morning. They are not good playmates. In reality they are basically stupid animals. So enjoying them as part of a Sunday dinner didn't bother me.

But ducks . . . ducks are a different story.

I was nine years old that year—the Easter of 1959. Murphy's displayed a new wrinkle in seasonal marketing—a second live display—this one full of baby ducks.

Are baby ducks cuter than baby chickens? I thought so. Are baby ducks smarter than baby chickens? I thought so. At least they could swim.

So that Easter, I purchased two ducklings. I was excited. In our photo album, there is a grainy black-and-white picture of our old family dog, his head resting on his paws, intently staring at two baby ducks paddling in a dishpan full of water.

Ducklings grow up pretty quick, and in a few short months they were no longer the tiny animals I could hold in an open palm, but fairly hefty birds with sleek white feathers. I took care of them. They were almost as loyal as my dog. They followed me around. I fed them cracked corn and duck feed, and they seemed to enjoy being petted.

I expanded the old chicken coop using scraps of old wood and chicken wire. Every Saturday I would reline their home with fresh straw. Ducks need to swim, so I buried my old wading pool at ground level. The ducks would spend hours in their little pool, paddling back and forth, back and forth.

One hot day that July, the gate to their pen must have been left open. The ducks were gone. I frantically searched the woods behind our house. They had taken a fifty-yard stroll and were happily swimming in a deep pool of Brush Creek. As they saw me coming, they must have realized the wrongness of their escape. They clamored out of the water, scrambled up the bank, and waddled back to their pen.

And every day after that first escape, I would feed them in the morning and change the water in their pool. They would eat a few bites, then slowly waddle through the gate and into the garden, looking for grubs and bugs. After a few minutes, the pair would set off for their workday at the creek.

Every evening around five, like clockwork, they would amble back up the hill to their pen and their evening meal. They were like two factory workers on their way home in the evening, punching in and punching out. The pair would go to the creek every day—except during winter when the creek was frozen.

In August of 1960, the ducks were more than a year old. It would be accurate to say that I was attached to them.

Our family was planning to make the annual trip to our summer cottage in Franklin, Pennsylvania, for a four-week stay. Since a large stream ran through that property, I was going to take my ducks with me. I had built a small pen, lined with straw, that fit snugly in the open trunk of our car.

It was the afternoon before we were to leave. The sky grew dark. With ominous echoes, thunder began to roll across the small valleys. A few flashes of lightning lit up the purple and darkening sky.

In the past, when a storm blew in, my ducks

23

would quickly waddle home from the creek to avoid the wind and rain.

This time, the violent storm crashed rapidly across the hills. The deluge hit the house like a train, and sheets of rain and wind crescendoed with the lightning and thunder. The storm sat above us for hours, shaking houses and uprooting trees.

It was well into the night before the rain and wind subsided.

Through the darkness, I looked out to the duck pen and realized they had not returned. It was too dark to search for them after the storm. I spent an anxious night in worry.

Early the following morning, I began to hunt for my pets. The creek was still swollen, filled to its banks with muddy, rushing water, higher than I had ever seen it before. I began to look downstream for my ducks, knowing that they could not have swum against the current for too long.

We would leave for vacation in a few hours, so I had little time.

A half a mile downstream and I saw nothing.

A mile downstream and I saw nothing.

Two miles downstream, the sun was climbing and time and real estate were running out. Within another half mile, Brush Creek empties into the main tributary of the Youghiogheny River, which winds past the rubber plant and the glass factory and the steel mills. This was before any of us ever knew anything about pollution control, but I knew that below that point the river was an open sewer for the factories, filled with ever-increasing levels of toxins and poisons and garbage and lead and acid.

This ten-year-old knew that if the ducks had been swept away past the joining point of the creek and the river, they would be gone.

I stood on the bank, scanning the river as it turned past the rubber factory. I looked and saw nothing. I knew that they were lost. I stood for a long time, waiting and watching and hoping. Then I turned and slowly trudged home.

What could I do?

Packing the car was not much fun that day. I had always looked forward to our vacations—but there was no joy in this day. The little pen I had built of wood and chicken wire was taken out of the car and put back into the garage.

I am sure they all tried to comfort me, but I didn't hear anything comforting. My ducks were gone and I was very, very sad.

The car was loaded, and we backed out of the driveway and went down the short gravel road to the highway. We turned right and drove the few hundred yards to the bridge over Brush Creek. My mother looked north—up the creek—and said, "Wait— what's that up the creek—by the quarry?"

I pressed my nose to the window and saw two tiny white specks against the blackness of the abandoned quarry—maybe half a mile upstream.

My dad pulled the car over to the side of the road, and I jumped out and ran as fast as I could. I realized that the ducks I had searched all morning for had been upstream instead of down.

As I got closer the ducks got more excited and animated. The night in the storm and wind and lightning had scared them too. They scrambled up the bank to meet me halfway. They were very relieved to see me.

It was a good day after all.

We got the ducks into their traveling pen and had a great vacation in the mountains. The ducks seemed to enjoy it too—happily swimming in the cold, clear, mountain stream.

As much as I loved those ducks, I couldn't protect them from the storm that night. But there is someone who can protect from the sudden storms we face. And that someone is God.

When he loves us, we are never lost—even if the storms of life drive us into places we thought not possible. And sometimes we'll find that the place of safety is a place we never anticipated being in. But rest assured—God's safety zone is far away from the toxins and garbage of the world.

Did God really protect my two pets that night and provide them safe harbor during the storm? I don't know. I'm not a theologian. But that ten-year-old boy knew in his heart that God had given them refuge.

I spent years searching through life for the "truth," and I have found the answer to most of life's complex questions to be amazingly simple. I like simple things. And once I learned an enduring truth from the most simple of teachers: those two white ducks.

You know, having learned some tough lessons

from experience, I can say that God's place of refuge
is more often upstream than downstream. The Christian life is often a story of struggling upstream to
safety, rather than easily floating downstream to
suffer from the poisons of the world.

I look back, and the image of those ducks is perfectly preserved in memory forever—two perfectly
white ducks slowly swimming against the blackness
of the slag and rubble of the old quarry. That's how
Christians should be seen in this world. Innocence
and purity will always be visible against a background of darkness and despair. And by being different, one becomes a beacon—a landmark. When
others are searching, they will be able to find us.
What we must do is be visible against the world—
but that means we must be in the world to be seen.

And what about my two ducks?

We kept them for another year until they were
adopted by a farmer who lived several miles upstream.
He liked duck eggs, he said. The pair lived on that
farm for the rest of their lives, laying eggs and safely
swimming in calm, clean waters.

Four

The Invitation

*He will wipe every tear from their eyes. There will
be no more death or mourning or crying or pain,
for the old order of things has passed away.
(Revelation 21:4)*

I was invited! It was wonderful news. It was perfect
news.

It was the summer of 1963. I had finished the
sixth grade. In western Pennsylvania, seventh grade
marked the start of junior high—different teachers,
different classes, different school.

Thirteen years old—the time that nature makes all

young boys . . . edgy. Confused. Driven . . . with absolutely no sense of direction.

As a teenager, our home was in Jeannette, just on the outskirts of town. To get to our home, you took a hard right off Oakford Park Road, up fifty yards of a steeper road. At the crest of the hill, you turned left into our driveway. Turn right, and two hundred yards farther there was another small cluster of homes. At the top of the hill was a bi-level home built of tan brick. In its day, it was "modern."

Lexene Lycette lived there.

Lexene was a year younger than I was and a year behind me in school. She was a pretty girl, with long black hair, dark eyes, and a soft and delicate manner. Hers was the pure and haunting beauty of a twelve-year-old. Every morning for three years, she waited for the yellow rumbly school bus with me and three other kids from the neighborhood. She would talk quietly with her younger sister and gently kick at small rocks until the bus arrived. I would sit as far back in the bus as possible. She always sat up front, one or two seats behind the driver.

Every three days her home was visited by the milkman and the truck that delivered Bunny Bread. The side of the bright yellow delivery van had a huge cartoon rabbit painted on it holding a loaf of Bunny Bread. I remember wanting to get our bread from the Bunny Bread man and have him carry the loaves right up to the house, just like at Lexene's house. But since my dad owned a retail bakery, it was not a wish that could ever be fulfilled.

The Invitation

It was the summer of 1963. A time to play kick-the-can in the fading warm twilight. It was a time to hike and camp out in the woods behind our home.

I was looking forward to our annual four-week vacation at our cabin in the mountains, two hours north of Jeannette. It had a swimming pool and a fishing stream and endless woods to hike and explore. Dad would join us for the first week and then weekends for the rest of our time there.

One day late in June, ten days before we were to leave on our trip, I went to pick up our mail. The mailbox was at the bottom of the hill, on the main road. I seldom got any mail, but I always volunteered to make the trip to the mailbox—just in case. On this day, there was a small tan envelope in the box—with my name on it. The address was written carefully, in slow, practiced, youthful strokes.

I quickly tore it open.

It was an invitation from Lexene—my neighbor Lexene—the object of my schoolboy crush. She had invited me to her birthday party on Saturday night. I was astonished. I was awestruck.

If *I* was invited, then this must be . . . a girl-boy party. It was the first one I had ever been invited to. Of course I am discounting any pre–first-grade celebrations which may or may not have been coed affairs.

A girl-boy party and I was invited. That meant that Lexene, who I almost never had the nerve to actually talk with, didn't think I was a total jerk.

A girl-boy party. This wasn't just good news, this

was BIG news . . . this was GREAT news . . . this was front-page extra edition news.

I was excited.

The rest of that week was sort of a blur as I mentally prepared for the event. I remember thinking and rethinking my wardrobe, planning and revising it a dozen times. I practiced combing my hair so it would look like the hair of the oldest son on *My Three Sons*. Now *he* was the essence of teenage cool and sophistication. My hair never quite matched his, but I tried. A little dab of Brylcreem did not do the wonders that it promised on TV.

I dressed very carefully the evening of the party. I may have even polished my shoes. It was starting to drizzle slightly, so I borrowed my older brother's sleek black umbrella, the kind that would flap open with the push of a button. I was ready. I was primed. I was wearing cologne. It was either Hai Karate or English Leather—or perhaps a lethal combination of the two.

I walked out into the mist and rain and slowly walked up the hill, careful not to get muddy. I didn't want to have to take my shoes off and go in my socks for the whole evening. I didn't imagine that girls would appreciate that.

As I approached Lexene's house, I began to feel more and more uneasy, unsettled down in my stomach. I was nervous, to be sure, but I was made more nervous because I didn't see anyone else arriving during my walk up the hill.

Was Lexene playing some sort of joke on me? Where were all the guests?

I got to her house and . . . just stood under the black umbrella in the darkening rain, in the middle of the red shale road, trying to make sense of it. I looked down the hill, and no cars were arriving. I looked toward the house and saw no lights on. I heard no laughter or music.

I stood there for what I thought was an eternity, waiting for someone else to arrive, someone to make the party real. Actually, I am sure I stood in that rain no more than a minute, when Lexene's dad opened the screen door and called out to me.

"Are you here for the party?"

I looked about and nodded.

"It's next Saturday, not tonight," he explained.

"Oh," I answered, confused. Had I really read the date wrong? With a sudden flash of awareness, I realized that I must have. "OK," I answered. "I guess I'll see you next week then."

The evening had gone black and cold.

And as I walked back down the hill, I realized with a sudden thud to my chest that I wouldn't be at home next week. We would be on vacation. I would miss the first girl-boy party of my life. Who knew if there would ever be another?

The good news that the invitation had held just a few minutes before had . . . evaporated, disappeared in an instant . . . right before my eyes.

That year, vacation was not quite as much fun as it had been in the past. I guess I had an OK time, but that first Saturday night, as I sat by the stream and watched fireflies paint the sky with their faint glow, as I watched shooting stars flash in the distant darkness, I knew that I was missing the social event of the summer.

The good news of that invitation—well—it wasn't good. It turned what should have been a wonderful vacation into a bitter taste at the back of my tongue.

Why couldn't the party have been a week earlier? Or why couldn't our vacation have been a week later? Why couldn't I talk my parents into letting me take a Greyhound bus home for the party?

The party came and went and I wasn't there. It was a brutal disappointment in my early social life.

Over the years, I am glad to report, I received other invitations—and some of them actually were to girl-boy parties. But regardless of the affair, none of them ever matched the magnitude of the experience that I imagined I missed at Lexene's party. I have yet to receive an invitation with so much anticipation, so much excitement.

That does seem to be the way of the world. Expectation never matches the reality. The gifts under the Christmas tree, still wrapped, are always more exciting, more satisfying, than the pile of merchandise that results by tearing off the wrappings. But there is one gift—one invitation, however—that will never disappoint. It is Christ's invitation to us to join him in heaven. That is the one invitation everyone is able to accept and is the only one that will never disappoint.

To be truthful, God's invitation to us is in our mailbox every day. Every day we have the opportunity to open it and accept it.

Five

Broken
Promises

*All of you know the truth. I do not write to you
because you do not know the truth, but because
you do know it and because no lie comes from
the truth. (1 John 2:20-21)*

I have never bought a hand buzzer or itching powder
or pepper gum or the fly in the fake ice cube or black
soap. I never liked the exploding snakes in the can or
whoopie cushions. This aversion to practical jokes
started a long time ago, in a more innocent time.

I was eight years old during the summer of 1958,
and the days had gone warm and soft. The summer

furniture had been hauled out from the basement to the flagstone patio by our back door. There were a couple of chairs and a hammock—and a glider sat right under the kitchen windows.

Do they still make gliders?

A glider is sort of a combination rocking chair, couch, and swing. It would glide back and forth, with very little arc involved, sort of a nontilting rocking chair sofa. And if you lay down on it, which was ideal on quiet summer afternoons, and hooked your feet under the arms and flexed, it would rock and glide in two directions, making a very pleasing squeaking noise as it lulled you into drowsiness.

When my father came home from work at his bakery around noon or so, he would often sit there on the green metal glider with the green-and-white vinyl upholstery. After lunch he would light up a cigar, listen to the radio, and perhaps nap, the cigar smoke hovering over his head like a halo.

My brother and I would enjoy this summertime ritual and his tales of the day's work. My father was a great storyteller, creating involved and complicated tales of who did what at work. His stories of work and relationships with his employees were either comical masterpieces or tragic vignettes.

My father truly enjoyed being the center of attention, telling the joke, being in the limelight. And he loved to play practical jokes on the people he worked with. And they played them back on him.

One of his favorite stories was the time when one of the bakers slipped a handful of salt into Dad's coffee a couple of times in a row. Working in a bakery,

36

with huge bins containing several hundred pounds of salt and sugar and flour, well, it wasn't too difficult to take a healthy pinch of something or other and slip it into a mug of coffee.

Putting stuff into other people's coffee cups was a big part of their repertoire of practical jokes. And coffee was a very important element in the lives of the bakers—when you go to work at 2 A.M., you need all the help you can get to stay awake.

The baker who had successfully performed the "salt and coffee" routine on my father was gloating. And wary. He kept his coffee in view at all times, carrying it with him to guard against retaliation.

The unspoken rule of the shop was that if you emptied a bin of flour or sugar, you had to go and replace it, climbing down the steep stone steps into the basement and returning with a hundred-pound bag perched on your bent shoulder.

My dad emptied a bin and went for the replacement. He emptied another and went for that also. Nothing out of the ordinary. The other baker poured a new cup of coffee and scooped out some sugar from the bin, stirred it into the hot liquid, and took a very large drink—immediately followed by running to the sink to spit it out.

My dad had spent the last few hours rearranging the bins, pouring the sugar into the empty salt bin, the salt into the sugar bin—all to get even.

He could be pretty focused.

One fretless summer afternoon, with a warm breeze lulling the air, the radio echoing from the kitchen, we gathered on the patio to listen to my

37

father finish his report of the day's news. He finished, lit a cigar, and added a very surprising footnote. He was buying an airplane from someone he had met at the barbershop.

An airplane?

To an eight-year-old, the prospect of having an airplane in the family was pretty gosh-darned amazing and wondrous. If you knew my father, it sounded normal. He would do stuff like that. He had in the past. He bought a used trampoline from a guy he met in that same barbershop, and we installed it just off the side yard. It was great, dangerous fun.

But an airplane? It never dawned on me that it was impractical—no one we knew had learned how to fly, and I knew my father was not the type to go for flying lessons. Anything more complex than a screwdriver intimidated him. He often said that if you couldn't fix it with a hammer or screwdriver, then it was good and broken.

All I knew is that he said we were getting an airplane. And I was ready for it. I could impress the bejeebers out of all my friends. I could learn to fly. You could get a pilot's license at fourteen—two years earlier than a driver's license.

Dad went on at length about the arrangements, what airfield we would use, where the hangar was, what color the plane was painted. It was great.

I spent that afternoon imagining the thrill of flying and the fabulous places this plane would take us. Disneyland! The Grand Canyon! Cape Canaveral! The freedom from the bonds of gravity. The freedom to go anywhere, to head off into the sky.

Later that night, the family was gathered informally on the patio after dinner. Conversation was quiet. The evening was cool and comfortable. I was inside the house. I went into the bathroom just off the kitchen. Its one high window opened up onto the backyard patio. Voices echoed cleanly into the dark room.

I heard my Dad say, "And he really thinks I'm going to buy an airplane. Jimmy fell for it hook, line, and sinker." And he laughed.

There was no sound as my carefully constructed world collapsed. The world with the airplane lay crumbled and smashed before that eight-year-old boy. I felt the tight tears of embarrassment come, mixed with a reddening shame for being taken in. I stayed there in the dark bathroom for a long time.

I never said another word about that airplane, never asked about it, never told anyone what I had heard that evening. I made a vow that I would never get caught like that again. I felt humiliated, taken advantage of, foolish.

This is the one reason that to this day I cannot tolerate practical jokes. I just can't take part in them. And I can't watch *Candid Camera*. I remember all too well how horrible it feels to suddenly realize that a promise has been broken. That a person you have trusted implicitly has violated that trust.

This is just a very small, nontraumatic episode. Magnify it a thousand times for the really big promises and the really horrible breaks of trust.

We all want to trust so much, and we so often trust the wrong person or trust in the wrong way.

39

Man, as we know from practical experience, as well as from the Bible, is untrustworthy and incredibly fallible.

It is hard for us to trust. And when people fail us and lie to us, we find it all that much more difficult to ever commit our hearts and our hopes to someone else.

But there is someone who does warrant our trust— God. Trusting is the same as having faith in God. The fact that God has never failed us should help convince us that he is indeed trustworthy.

Someday I may get over my intolerance of practical jokes. But I know how important promise keeping is. That much my father taught me—perhaps in a way he never imagined.

Six

A Winter's Tale

*Blessed is he who has regard for the weak; the
Lord delivers him in times of trouble. The Lord will
protect him and preserve his life. (Psalm 41:1-2)*

Learning about God is often best learned through
practical experience. The Bible tells us that God has
protective arms, but I have yet to see any celestial
limbs reaching down from the skies. There was a
time though, as a ten-year-old boy, when I felt them.
Maybe not God's arms exactly, but I knew then what
it must feel like to be in his protective, encompassing
embrace.

A few weeks before Christmas of 1960, my oldest brother, Fred, returned home from the army on holiday leave. Stationed at a veterans hospital in New Orleans, he served as an orderly and emergency room technician.

Fred was twenty-four and I was ten. He was tall with a deep, head-tilted-back, booming laugh. He always made me laugh—though I didn't always know what it was we were laughing at. He was an artist and a magician, amazing me with sleight-of-hand stunts and card tricks. Our age difference meant that we never went on bike rides together or went hiking or camping in the woods. Fred was in high school as I strain to remember the first real memory I have that includes his face.

But there was one incident . . . one time . . . when he was no longer an older brother, but a magic person who saved lives and protected little boys, especially during one time of tough sledding. One cold and dark December night will live forever in my mind. In western Pennsylvania during winter, darkness swallows the valleys by midafternoon.

Since I grew up in the hills of western Pennsylvania, it was all but mandatory to ride sleds in the winter. It actually might have been the state law for all children to go sledding to build strength, endurance, and courage. You needed all three attributes in abundance for the infamous Number 17. Number 17 was the premier sledding hill in all of Westmoreland County—the seventeenth hole at the Greensburg Country Club.

Number 17 was a par-three hole, the tee located at

the very top of the highest point on the golf course. A good eight-iron shot would easily carry from tee to green, a distance of around 175 yards on the horizontal plane. But a golf ball on the seventeenth would travel the 175 yards out while plummeting about 500 yards down.

A well-groomed hill and virtually vertical from a ten-year-old's perspective, it thankfully had a huge landing area at the base of the hill that offered the illusion of distant safety.

Making the ride more interesting, the hill featured a series of sand traps and pine trees square in the middle of the fairway. They presented a major danger to tobogganers, who lack the rudiments of steering control. To sledders, they were just scenery.

The ride down was devilish—straight down and panic inducing. Most of our sledding was done at night, when the moon stole the colors from our vision and the trips became a black and white abstraction, a surreal vision of speed and danger and snow and cold and dark.

It was late December, the twenty-third, a Friday night, early evening. My three older brothers, Fred, Bob, and Tim, decided it was sledding time. Clothing and equipment were gathered from closets and cedar chests. My sled of choice was an old, battered, hill-scarred Flexible Flyer. The varnish on the wooden slats was gone, and the red, ornate painted logo reduced to ghost letters, rubbed smooth by years of snowsuit friction. Bob, the family mechanic, took my sled, sanded the runners clean, heated them with his small, blue tanked blowtorch till they reached a dull

43

orange glow and then, with paraffin borrowed from my mother's canning supplies, hissed the wax across the runners till they gleamed with the promise and threat of dangerous speed.

We piled into Bob's 1946 Dodge two-door coupe. He was in the process of customizing it. The original paint was laboriously ground off and replaced with several coats of flat gray primer. Bob always had a case of spray paint in the garage—all flat gray primer. This was the apex of most of his customizing plans. A whole series of gray cars were parked in our driveway that decade.

In a few minutes, we reached the seventeenth hole and quickly sprinted up the hill and made our first few runs in the crackling cold.

Several trips later I stood at the summit of Number 17, under the full moon, watching others descend down the smooth, pearl white snow. A dozen or so older riders, teenagers, both boys and girls, stood giggling around a long and unwieldy toboggan. They jockeyed for position, vying for the right location to achieve the proper girl-boy combinations. They all sat, giggling and whispering, and slowly, a swarm of arms extended from the mass of riders like the oars of a Viking ship, and in practiced unison, they pushed against the snow-packed ground. The death-sled toboggan slowly began to inch into the pitch of the hill.

I let it glide away a second or two, and then I picked up my sled, cradled it in my arms, jumped to the snow, and began my run, following them. I planned to zoom past them in a cloud of snow dust, adding a thrill to an already terrifying trip. We both picked up speed. The tobogganers began their chants of "lean" and "lean right" and "lean left."

I pulled beside the toboggan, ready to terrorize them. And then, something unexpected happened. For a brief moment, they all leaned together— toward me. Having twelve screaming teenagers plunging toward your sled is not pleasant, but it was a simple matter to push the right steering strut forward, pull the left back, veering safely and quickly from their path.

They forced me onto the more northerly side of the hill, a little steeper, a little faster, and a little farther from the green. *Great ride,* I thought to myself, the cold night air bringing tears to my eyes as I plummeted downward.

I should have played golf there in the summer, when the snow didn't hide obstacles. At the very bottom of this side of the hill was a drainage ditch— six inches deep and two feet across—to carry rain water away from the green. This was the rough to the golfers. I am sure it came into play infrequently. And I didn't know of its existence.

That is, until a few seconds later.

The nose of my Flexible Flyer ducked slightly as it entered the ditch. I followed it, nose to nose, forehead to metal frame. And in another brief instant, the nose of the sled slammed into the opposite side of the ditch and pinwheeled over and over. The two of us, sled and rider, were one as we arced into the night. With a muffled thump I came to a stop in a heap, on my back, facing the sky. My sled skittered off into the distance and came to rest near the road. My breath came in short puffs, little clouds of mist rising toward the sky.

Have you ever made snow angels in the deafening quiet of an empty field under the iridescent spotlight of a full moon? When it is so still that you can hear the snowflakes as they fall and tumble against each other? On my back, lying there, I looked up into the cold inkiness of the December night, into the stars that filled the sky. In that torn fragment of a moment, I felt a true sense of peace.

Then, as the adrenaline began to pump throughout my body, I realized that I was seeing the stars with monocular vision. There was only one eye operating. I began to wail. I was blinded. My eye was gone. I was going to die.

Fifty yards away, on the seventeenth green, heads snapped in my direction. They peered into the darkness to locate the source of the screaming.

In another moment, I saw darker silhouettes against the sky as figures gathered around to peer down at me. I saw a flicker of light. It was Johnny Modar, faithful chrome-plated Zippo lighter in hand. He was a Marlboro man back then. I heard a voice. "Jeez, look at all that blood."

That wasn't what I wanted to hear.

In the same moment, my brother Fred, fresh from his army hospital duties, knelt beside me. He pulled my hat off and used a handful of snow to wipe away the blood that was pouring into my right eye.

"Head wounds are bleeders," he said, "but they usually aren't serious."

Usually wasn't a word I wanted to hear.

In that flickering light from Johnny's lighter, Fred tended to my wound. I heard other voices—cautious, low, confidential mutterings. "Do you think we need an ambulance?" someone asked.

Ambulance wasn't a word I wanted to hear.

A handkerchief was placed over the cut and held firmly. The nose of my sled had caught me at eyebrow height, digging to the bone in the soft flesh. Blood was pouring from the wound, blinding me.

Fred gently pushed his arms beneath me in the snow and scooped me up and carried me, limp, and no doubt still wailing, into Bob's gray 1946 Dodge coupe.

As he walked the hundred yards to the car carrying me, I knew that I was safe. The gash on my head throbbed and pulsed, but I was safe. My heart raced, but I had arms around me that kept the fear and darkness away. Nothing in my life since then has matched that feeling of going from indescribable terror to feeling safe and secure in an instant.

It was real . . . palpable . . . physical . . . and I could feel the safety deep in my soul.

That is how I envision the arms of God—warm, safe, eternally secure. When I accepted God's gift of salvation, and God bent down to lift me to him and to wrap his arms around me, I was pulled from the cold blackness and blinding terror of death into the loving arms of God and eternal life.

That is what it feels like. A ten-year-old filters out very little and feels everything. As we get older, we filter out more and more, and we get better and better at denying what we feel and what we need. As a child, hurt, scared, and lying in the cold and dark, I needed my brother's arms to make me feel secure and protected and safe.

As an adult, living in the cold darkness of the world, I often need God's arms around me. I call out to him to save me from my tears and my pain. At times I sense him kneeling to pick me up, just as my brother did more than twenty years ago. God's arms are so much safer, so much more secure. His safety, love, and protection are available to all of us who call on him.

Seven

Death Denied

*Show me, O Lord, my life's end and the number
of my days; let me know how fleeting is my life.
You have made my days a mere handbreadth;
the span of my years is as nothing before you.
Each man's life is but a breath. (Psalm 39:4-5)*

You climb a tree thirty feet in the air, and just as
your sneakers lose their grip on a moss-covered
branch, you reach up and grab the loose and rotting
branch above you and swing, with wood creaking
and breaking, to a sturdier and drier branch. As you
grapple for this limb with your feet, your handhold

gives way, and with a sudden lurch you wrap arms and legs around the live branch. You turn your head and watch with pounding heart as the dead branch breaks off and plummets to the ground, with bits of bark fluttering after it. You count the seconds . . . one, two, three, four, five . . . and then a *WHUMP* as it explodes against the ground in a shower of leaves and forest dust.

That's cheating death—something most of us experienced often as we were growing up.

Or the time you were playing under the railway bridge a mile from home, hunting for crayfish in the still waters of Jack's Run. It is summer and the sun is hot and home is too far away, so you bend down and take a long drink near the spillway of the small concrete dam. You are unaware that the creek carries sewage from the strip mine and the homes farther up the creek. But you do not get sick. The water, contaminated everywhere else on the creek, was clean from where you drank.

That's cheating death.

Or the time you rode your sled down the very steep Woodlawn Avenue in your neighborhood at twilight. You scoot through the intersection, unaware that a car, speeding down the hill, misses crushing you and your sled by mere seconds. It is so close that the driver has nightmares as he recalls the incident years later.

That's cheating death.

Death has been denied each time. Yet in your childhood innocence, it never registers, never seems real. Children don't consider death an option, or even a possibility.

As I experienced each of these brushes with mortality, death never entered my mind. It was not that death only happened to others—it was that death never happened at all.

That is, until that chilled and dark Friday afternoon, three days before Christmas, in 1961.

Christmas was a special time at our house. My father owned a retail bakery, and the few weeks before any major holiday were a whirl of special orders and long hours in front of the ovens, baking strudels and breads and German delicacies. I helped when I could, spending days folding white bakery boxes of various sizes along the creases, inserting tabs into slots, bending lids, so the sales clerks would have a stack of ready-made containers when the crush of shoppers descended on the store.

The bakery was always a frenzy of activity and work the week of Christmas. The three or four days before Christmas dictated twenty-hour days for my father and his crew. They barely had enough time for a shower, a quick nap, and a snack during the entire Christmas week. It was brutal work, and I felt sorry for my father as he toiled.

Christmas was marked by insufferable waiting for the opening of gifts. My brother Tim and I waited, bored and alone since both our parents were at work most of the week. We looked forward to having the rest of the family gathered at home for the celebrations.

My oldest brother, Fred, would be returning in a few days from art college in Philadelphia. Bob was on his way home from baking trade school in Minneapolis. My sister Louise was attending a teachers college in Indiana, Pennsylvania, and was due home from her student teaching assignment.

It was a time to be a whole family once again.

I was home alone that day, Tim was at the bakery, and it was my job to wait for my sister and welcome her home. I stared out the window in the living room. I could see the road wind away through the thicket of trees, the view usually blocked from sight by leaves and foliage. Louise would be driving her white Dodge Dart, the kind with the push-button gear selectors built into the dashboard.

Westmoreland County was quieted that day by a heavy wrapping of snow. It piled up in the branches of trees, covered the small streams, and filled in the noisy spaces in the world with snow's quiet, muffling silence. The county did not plow as often then, nor use much salt. As a result, the secondary roads were often white with a hard, snow-packed surface. Driving could be treacherous.

And the road to our house was even worse. It was a steep unpaved incline, perhaps fifty yards up to our driveway with a hard right, ninety-degree turn to the paved road. I do not think our road was ever plowed. The snow was just packed and rutted by us and our neighbors.

This last incline would often defeat the most savvy driver. One would start seventy-five yards down the paved road to build up speed, do a controlled slide onto the unpaved road, violently slam the wheels back and forth, bounce in and out of ruts, and then slide sweetly into our driveway.

Our hill-climbing attempts were not always success-ful. Two, three, and sometimes four tries were made before we climbed the summit or admitted defeat by parking the car at the bottom of the hill. There was always a plowed area just in front of the fence that protected a gas-company pumping substation.

I sat in the growing darkness of our living room, watching the shadows creep from the ridge to the west and spill across the narrow valley. I would count the cars as they passed out of view. I would tell myself that my sister would be in the twelfth car that passed, and as the thirteenth rumbled by, I would add another dozen to my prediction.

I waited in the twilight and counted, with the family dog, Mumbo, at my side.

Mumbo was an inappropriate name for such a noble dog. She was named after a song that was pop-ular in the mid-fifties, or so I am told. She was born of a stray who had her pups behind the gas station down the road from our home. The owner took a torn piece of cardboard box and taped it on the front window of the station. In black crayon, the sign read: Free Puppies. I remember peering over the edge of a frayed and oil-stained cardboard box and seeing it alive with bouncing puppies, crawling and yawn-ing and tumbling. I remember winding the loudly ticking clock that the puppy would sleep with for comfort that first lonely night apart from her family, to hear the ticking as a substitute for her mother's heartbeat.

She was, without a doubt, the finest dog a boy could have. I have in my photo collection a black-

and-white snapshot of me, age seven or so, asleep on a small wicker couch, my back facing the camera. I have my arm wrapped over the dog, who was wedged in the small space between me and the couch back. The dog looks clearly uncomfortable, but her eyes indicate that if this is where her master is, then this is where she should be. My mother tells me that she stayed there for hours that evening as I slept.

She was a fireplug of a dog, with black wiry hair and a splash of brown at her muzzle, throat, and paws. She was smart, loyal, and incredibly enthusiastic.

Mumbo and I waited as dusk settled closer to night. Then, through the faint light, I saw a familiar white car slow down and signal a right turn.

It was my sister, and I ran to get my coat. Mumbo was up and excited as I was, though I am sure she did not know why.

Louise tried to climb the hill to our house, and halfway up the tires began to spin and whine and smoke. Into reverse and back onto the highway for one more try. By this time, I was out the door and the dog was right behind me. Louise tried one more time and made it no higher than halfway. She was intimidated by snow and parked at the bottom of the hill, maneuvering her car to the level spot in front of the gas company's fence.

Mumbo and I sat just below our driveway on a small rock outcropping. Twenty-five yards down the steep embankment was the road. Our breath misted in the cold air. The white car stopped, the brake lights flashed once and then blinked off as the motor was switched off. It was quiet. I could hear the ticking of the hot engine in the cold winter air. It sounded loud.

The door slowly opened, and Louise stepped out into the cold December air, her breath making little clouds. I waved and she waved back, a big smile on both our faces. Suddenly Mumbo realized who this person was. Cars meant nothing to her. It was the people that she recognized. And this was a person who lived in her house, who was part of the family and needed to be met in person. Mumbo gave a bark or two of welcome. She wagged her tail in joy and anticipation. In an instant she took off down the hill to meet this one who hadn't been here in weeks and weeks and weeks.

I watched as the scene began to unfold in slow motion. I leaned to the left an inch or two. I could hear the very faint rumbling of another approaching car. It was closer than I realized, the snow muffling the tires on the road.

Not only was the dog running in slow motion, it was as though I was apart from the scene, observing it from a distance, seeing myself and my sister and my dog all at the same time. Louise looked up the hill to see Mumbo running toward her, happy and grinning and wiggling with excitement. I looked to the south and saw the car, now just coming into view, only seconds from the two of them. The car was not speeding, traveling perhaps thirty-five miles per hour on the slippery road.

I saw Louise put her hand to her mouth in terror.

I called—no, screamed—for the dog to stop, but

55

all she knew was that this was someone who had to be greeted.

There was a terrifying geometry of sights to this moment. Mumbo bounded onto the road at the exact second that the car entered the same space. At one end of this triangle is my sister, her eyes wide and white with shock. At the far end of the triangle is an eleven-year-old boy who is seeing his best friend disappear beneath the front end of a car. There is a geometry of sounds as well, the sound of my sister's terrified scream, the silent, angry hiss of the car's tires as they bite for traction in the densely packed snow, the soft, almost feminine slide as the car shudders to a stop twenty yards from the bridge over Brush Creek, and finally, the silent sob of a small boy whose vision has given way to tears.

I had just witnessed the death of perhaps my closest friend in the world, who accepted me as I was, with never a judgment, with never a criticism. A massive, throat-closing lump formed, and my chest constricted in pain. I turned away, praying, hoping, crying out to God that this was just a bad dream, that it never really happened, that I would wake in just a moment.

An eternity passes, and the driver of the car is out and walking to my sister and saying that he didn't mean it, that he wasn't going that fast, that he could not have stopped in time or swerved to miss the dog. His voice is wavering. I know that he is not to blame.

At that instant I saw how tenuous life was and how I should have guarded my friend better. The tears are flowing, and the sobs come and shake my body with a force all their own.

But then . . . just then . . . there is another noise in that dark and silent evening. There is a yelp of sorts, a whine, a soft bark. And then, a moment later, a black nose peeks out from underneath the car, and slowly, gingerly, my dog crawls out onto the snow-packed road. He looks at my sister for a moment, he looks at the car behind him, and then, with a bit of a wobble, he runs back into my arms.

In a retrospective ranking, this was perhaps the second or third most glorious moment in my life. But at that moment, it was the essence of all life, the culmination of all possible joys. It was the universe and the reason for life all rolled into the one, most brilliant, pellucid moment ever experienced by anyone.

Mumbo huddled back into my arms, looking every bit as terrified as I was. Her back was stained with grease, her coat was covered with snow and road grime, but she was alive. The snow had allowed her to slide, the locked wheels missing her by inches, and they had slid as a unit, car and dog beneath, on the snow-packed road. Exactly how it happened, I will never know. Perhaps God cupped his hand around that small black dog and allowed her to live.

The three of us—me, my sister, and the driver of the car—looked at each other in that empty way that people do when they have witnessed a miracle. Each of us knew that there were no words available to truly describe the event. Even now, as I recall those moments, I realize that these words offer a pale imitation of the reality of that event. I saw firsthand the fragility of life and the miracle of a life spared that cold winter's afternoon.

Seeing death face-to-face was painful. I suppose that making us have to deal with death as human beings is perhaps God's way of telling us what he faced as he watched his own Son's death. Later, much later in my life, a day finally came when I understood the magnitude of God's great gift to us in the birth and then the death of his Son.

I see another geometric triangle: God's Son hanging on a cross; then the laughing mob, the very people for whom he was giving his life; and a Father watching from heaven as his Son dies, heartbroken over our sins and the price being paid to redeem us.

There was another lesson for me that day—of how fragile life really is and how every day is a gift from God, something to enjoy each moment as best we can, remembering that each moment is precious.

Eight

Doctrinal
Errors

or

That Isn't the Way You Spell *Avuncular*

*And here you yourself must be an example to
them of good deeds of every kind. Let everything
you do reflect your love of the truth and the fact
that you are in dead earnest about it. Your conversation should be so sensible and logical that anyone who wants to argue will be ashamed of
himself because there won't be anything to criti-
cize in anything you say! (Titus 2:7-8, TLB)*

How does a nontheologian illustrate the problem
of following the examples of other Christians
rather than following the example of Christ? An

incident from seventh grade made the point clearly.

Benevolent
Scurrilous
Avuncular
Gregarious
Turbulent

Does this enumeration of definitions annunciate a sentient person of your acquaintance? If so, it is a serendipitous circumstance. Please, if you would, perdure, and ultimately the import of these words will be elucidated in a pellucid manner.

Softly now, as we walk past Mr. Arthur's seventh-grade English class at Harold Junior High School. It is late in the afternoon. The frenzy of the morning has given way to a calmer time, an almost peaceful period. Stop by the half-open door. Lean in to hear the murmur and hesitant melody of 30 seventh graders softly repeating words and their definitions to themselves. Their voices are just barely audible. It was as if you stumbled onto a living dictionary, each student preserving a portion of the big book, matching word to definition.

That was Mr. Arthur's way of educating his young charges. Words were the key. Vocabulary was the key. Expansion of language was the key. Mr. Arthur loved the English tongue and worshiped at the feet of Webster and Roget.

At least that's what we thought.

Mr. Arthur, a very quiet, controlled teacher with a

curled wave of black hair and thick, black-framed glasses, given to few emotional outbursts, was the seminal figure for a generation of literate seventh graders in his small corner of the educational world.

Two aspects of seventh-grade English will be forever etched in my memory. The first was the diagramming of sentences, a practice so curious, so oddly byzantine, that I am not able to conjure more than a fleeting image of it to mind.

The second was vocabulary. Not just simple vocabulary, but a subset of vocabulary, populated and ruled by "flash cards." Flash cards, in a variety of types, are a standard in many disciplines. You can find them being used for training in math, foreign language, history, and most other types of academic activity.

But what made Mr. Arthur's flash cards unique and memorable was that they were student produced. Every Friday afternoon, we were given a blue mimeographed sheet of the week's words. We were required to cut used manila file folders into small, careful rectangles, one inch tall and two inches wide. We then transferred each vocabulary word to the front of one of the twenty-five or thirty fresh-cut cards. The definition was written on the flip side. We sat, dictionary in hand, and looked up each word.

The rest of the week we would drill—the word, the spelling, the meaning, all combined into a litany of definitions. The murmuring you heard outside Mr. Arthur's door would be the students, quietly testing themselves on the current batch of words.

The words at the beginning of this tale are courtesy of Mr. Arthur. I know them because he made us know them. Is there drama in vocabulary? Is there tragedy in seventh-grade English? The point and counterpoint to this tale can be summed up in two words: *Bob Jouret.*

Bob Jouret's parents owned a small TV, appliance, and furniture store around the corner from my father's bakery in Jeannette. From that store I bought my first tape recorder—a gray, bulky Grundig, weighing forty pounds and advertised as portable.

They were also the only family I knew of in Jeannette with a French-sounding name.

Bob was one year ahead of me in school. A tall, muscular kid, he excelled in sports, playing on the varsity ninth-grade squads as a seventh grader. He was famous, in a junior high way, by being taller and stronger than most everyone else.

I delivered the *Jeannette News-Dispatch* to their home five days a week. For seven cents (I kept two cents as my commission) you could read all about the local happenings. Occasionally I would see Bob there, cutting grass or sitting on the porch. We would talk in that truncated, staccato manner familiar to all junior-high-age kids.

"Hi."

"Hi."

"That today's paper?"

"Yeh. You cutting the grass?"

"Yeh."

"See ya."

"Yeh."

Not exactly Noël Coward, but many of our conversations stayed at that monosyllabic level. Perhaps this is one of the reasons for Mr. Arthur's manic approach to improving our level of speech.

To me, these dialogues constituted a relationship, a friendship with an upperclassman, and a famous upperclassman at that.

The school year at Harold Junior High had begun. I was a seventh-grade student now, learning how to change classes, learning how to adapt to different teachers, learning how to navigate the geography of a new school.

And now—flash cards as well. Cutting up thirty little squares of paper, transferring a single word to each, then flipping through the dictionary to find out what they meant. This ordeal could take upwards of an hour—an eternity to a seventh grader.

But this also exposed us as a class to a foretelling of the future, a time when more serious works would be bought and sold between students. It was our first taste of this peculiar educational black market. If you were lucky, your older brother or sister had Mr. Arthur's class. If so, you simply recycled their old flash cards. The words of Mr. Arthur changed precious little from year to year, perhaps a word or two at a time. If you weren't blessed with prudent siblings, one could do the next best thing—buy old flash cards from an upperclassman.

Thirty words a week times four weeks a month times seven months of school equaled 840 flash cards. That's a whole lot of cutting and writing and looking up words. Even then, I thought I had better things to do with my time.

It was during one of our scintillating conversations

(between Bob and me) when I was first exposed to this new venture, this new type of commerce.

"Who ja get for English?"

"Mr. Arthur."

"He's a jerk."

"Yeh."

"What about those flash cards?"

"Lotta words."

"Yeh. Want to buy my old cards?"

"Yeh? How much?"

"Five bucks."

Five dollars was a lot of money—more than a week's worth of paper route money. But it would save an immense amount of my time. And Bob was my friend.

"OK."

This was great. The next week, when the list came out, I folded up the paper and did other things in class that day. When I got home, I rummaged through the shoe box full of dog-eared and thumb-stained flash cards, each week carefully bundled with a rubber band. It took a few minutes to find the right week's worth of words, make sure that they were all there, and commence studying.

This was great. It was quick, easy, and painless.

That first Friday, as the tests came back, rippling down each row, from student to student, I was prepared. Most of Mr. Arthur's tests were multiple choice, matching word to definition.

Monday morning came and I got a 75 on the test. What? That was not expected at all. I was good in English. Maybe I just had an off day. Maybe I didn't study as hard or concentrate as much as I should have.

The second week I worked a bit harder, drilled a bit longer, and knew those words backwards and forwards.

Monday rolled around and there was a big red 76 staring me in the face. This wasn't right. I was a bright kid. Low grades were for other people, not me. In my head, a small warning buzzer hummed and then went off with a loud report. I needed to check something.

That night I went home and pulled out the current week's worth of words. Each word was done in Bob's slow, loopy scrawl that I was getting used to. I selected a card. I flipped open my dictionary. I thumbed through the pages to the right word. I slid my finger along the definition slowly, reading aloud. I turned the flash card over with an ominous foreboding.

Well . . . now here was a problem. The two definitions were not even close. One could have been a description of chickens and the other a description of the moon. Different dictionaries wouldn't have caused this gross discrepancy. I went through the entire stack. Seven out of the thirty were completely wrong. I went through the words of last week and the week before—probably one definition in five had no bearing to the word on the front.

I was stunned.

Maybe that's why Bob never did so well in Mr. Arthur's class.

It was an epiphany in my life. I had been misled. I had trusted Bob and his work. And it was all wrong.

I know he didn't do it on purpose nor knowingly, but he led me astray.

I never complained to him about his error-ridden cards or asked for money back. After all, he was a lot bigger than I was.

That afternoon, I put the lid on the shoe box containing all Bob's cards, walked to the trash can, and dumped them in, seeing five dollars go with them.

You know, that's the kind of thing that happens in our Christian life. It happens when we take other people's words as the ultimate truth. We believe what they say instead of taking the time to go to the source of the truth on our own.

I could have saved myself two nearly failing grades by going to the source of the truth myself. I recovered in seventh-grade English and graduated into eighth grade. I also learned an important academic lesson in researching the truth that year.

Funny, though, I never applied this lesson in researching the truth regarding God until much later. Some lessons are hard learned indeed.

Trying to buy the truth from someone else came with a serious price to one seventh grader. And it still does today.

Go to the source.

All too often, we look to other Christians to be our yardstick. We see them and say, "If they can do that, so can I." We see their actions or their words as setting boundaries for our words and our actions.

Going to the source is still the best way to maintain standards.

It's pellucid.

Nine

The Arc– Gunpowder and Blood

Therefore do not let sin reign in your mortal body so that you obey its evil desires. Do not offer the parts of your body to sin, as instruments of wickedness, but rather offer yourselves to God, as those who have been brought from death to life; and offer the parts of your body to him as instruments of righteousness. For sin shall not be your master, because you are not under law, but under grace. (Romans 6:12-14)

I was eager to pass through the summer of 1962, this last one of my childhood. I was anxious to

experience life as an adult, as a first-year teenager. I
wanted to grab on to new experiences and hold on tight.

It was during the liquid warmth of a July afternoon
that I learned the danger of holding on too long.

It was a short, explosive incident.

Twelve years old is a curious age. It is a time of
awakening. Deep within, there are the first stirrings
of volatile emotions. The soul is beginning to recognize the existence of the temptations of the flesh.
There is an acknowledgement of the reality of sin
and the fascinating evil that it entails. There is a
desire to taste the danger of life. At least there was
in this twelve-year-old.

For as long as I remembered, we spent summers
at our family cottage. The first cottage was on Lake
Erie. That was replaced by our cabin deep in the
woods of north-central Pennsylvania a dozen or so
miles south of Franklin and Oil City. It was a real log
cabin, built by a local doctor of some prominence,
situated deep in the woods beside a pristine mountain stream. Our property covered forty acres of
primeval forest. The cottage was shaded by huge
conifers and oaks, and in the field across the stream
was a swimming pool. We would spend our days
swimming, exploring in the woods, spotting deer
as they nimbled through the woods, watching the
falcons circle the fields.

And come the Fourth of July, we would engage
in the ritual of blowing things up with fireworks.

Fireworks were illegal in Pennsylvania and had
been for years. But somehow, our corner of the state
flouted this along with several other legal codes.

At the end of June, my father and my older brother Tim and I would walk down Clay Avenue several blocks to the south end of town, just across the railroad tracks. Our destination was the Jeannette Variety Store. It was tucked into a small storefront, offering an indiscriminate jumble of products. Everything from nylons to washing machines to hunting rifles was available. And at the end of June, when you asked for Sonny with a nod and a wink, you were escorted to the back room. Amid the clutter and stacked boxes, Sonny tended store. He stood by crates and crates of firecrackers, Roman candles, skyrockets, M-80s, sparklers, cherry bombs, bottle rockets, golden cascades—nearly everything under the sun that could be made with gunpowder.

My father and Sonny would speak in low tones, and Sonny would smile and begin to pick up packages of Black Cat firecrackers and Whistling Dixies. Soon a large paper grocery bag would be filled to the brim with controlled substances.

Each firecracker, each bottle rocket, each cherry bomb held the lure of illicit pleasure. My father grew up with these pleasures, and I imagine he still got a vicarious thrill from them. They were dangerous and he shouldn't have bought them for us, but he did.

We spent many a summer afternoon up at the cabin in Franklin blowing up pine cones, detonating mushrooms, exploding old tree stumps. We savored each small explosion, the way the noise echoed across the stream, the way the white smoke hung along the darkened forest floor.

Each year the cache of fireworks would be divided

69

equally between my brother Tim and myself. If the number of packs of fireworks happened to be an odd number, we unwrapped the last package and divided it by unwrapping the long strands of master fuse holding the individual ones in a string.

I was more impulsive than Tim. He would marshal out his fireworks very carefully and frugally. He would still have a bundle of firecrackers at the end of summer—mine would be all gone by nightfall on the Fourth. Tim may even have some old firecrackers still hidden away in the back of a dresser drawer.

Setting off these mini-explosions acted as a release. Any pent-up anger or hostility or frustration would be exploded along with the firecracker. It was a cathartic experience of sorts, even though this twelve-year-old had no idea of what *cathartic* meant. I just knew that it felt good to watch the explosions.

My older brother Bob was at the cabin on this day in 1962 and had a package of firecrackers of his own. He stood at the edge of the stone patio, the wall below trailing down to the stream. He stood that afternoon at the edge of the wall with a punk stick in one hand, its slowly burning ember coloring the air with its dense smell, and lit firecrackers.

Not just lit them—he practiced the art of explosion, the delicate balance of danger and beauty.

His left hand was held low, punk stick smoldering. His right hand would lightly hold the firecracker, its fuse extended. At the first fuse spark, and with a windmill arc of his right arm, he tossed the firecracker into the air. If all the actions were timed right—and with Bob, they often were—the firecracker would speed into the sky, its fuse smoking, and at the peak of the arc, the apex of its climb, it would explode in a shower of sparks and smoke and sound.

Magnificent, when done right.

The echo would drift away, and the thousand tiny bits of paper and wadding would flutter like wounded birds to the ground. The wind would drift away the smoke in gentle swirls.

My father watched and yelled out the window. "Don't do it that way. Set it on the ground. When you blow up your hand, you better not come crying to me."

My father was a wonderful man, but compassion was not his strong suit.

In a few short minutes, the show was over and my brother went on to other diversions. I stood at the patio edge, mentally reviewing the motions, the thrill, the sight, the sound.

I still had lots of fireworks. *I'll just get a small package of the little tiny fireworks. Maybe I'll try just one.* It did look like a lot of fun. I had never done this before and I was nervous.

I pulled the red waxy paper off the pack of forty-eight Black Cats and stuffed it in my pocket. I found the master string and tugged to the right and then left, unweaving the individual pieces. As I freed them from the string, I carefully laid them in a long row on the picnic table nearby.

I found a new punk stick. I struck a kitchen match and lit the punk stick, blowing on it to fire the ember to an orange glow.

With the punk stick in my left, a Black Cat in my right, I touched fuse and fire together. A spark sputtered out and I panicked, threw it down to the ground. It bounced over the wall and exploded in a small fury as it hit the ground below the patio wall.

I didn't blow up. I smiled to myself, heart thumping.

Let me try one more. At first spark I tossed it away and this one arced low and bounced to the ground, obviously a dud. Maybe it wasn't lit right, I said to myself. Maybe I have to hold it a bit longer to get it going.

The third one sparked, I arced my arm and in a beautiful blending of sound and fury, it exploded in midair, almost at the top of the arc.

The next several were much the same.

One more firecracker was lit and tossed. It arced up, and for one brief moment at the top of the curve, it hung there in midair as if suspended by a line. Before it began to return to earth, the fuse entered the tightly wound paper cylinder, the gunpowder began to mix oxygen and heat, and in a flash it expanded with a roar, its paper entrails streaming downward.

What beauty, I thought, *what grace.*

On the picnic table, the fuse of the next firecracker in line must have rubbed on the table. A grain or two of gunpowder leaked out. There was a crease in the fuse that shortened its burning time. The forces of nature conspired.

As I touched the punk to the fuse, it leaped toward its explosive charge a bit faster, a touch quicker than all the rest. I began my arc slower than before. I swung too far out to the left.

An inch out of my hand, as fingers released and spread open, the Black Cat class C fireworks device exploded as designed. The force of the blast spread my fingers out wider than before, and before I knew what I had done, I began screaming.

I am sure my father came out, but it was my mother I ran to first. She opened my palm, and at the tip of my thumb and at the tips of the first two fingers were blisters, evil and menacing, filled with darkened blood.

Blood blisters, my father called them.

My hand hurt as if I had picked up a red-hot poker.

"I told you so," my father shouted angrily several times as I grimaced in pain.

My wounds were iced, disinfected, and bandaged, and I spent the rest of that afternoon, and most of the next few days, reading and rereading comic books on the porch. My right hand truly ached for a week.

I learned some important lessons that day—about firecrackers and about life.

There are dangers in the illicit. There are dangers in that evil beauty. Hold on too long to something evil just because it feels good and the explosion will hurt you. I learned about the danger of sin. It looks like fun. It looks easy. It entices.

Ultimately sin will explode, and no power on earth will enable you to jerk your hand back from the blast in time. Hold on too long, too tight—hold on to the wrong pleasures—and it will happen to you.

I thought I was immune to the dangers of a firecracker. I took precautions. I was careful. It wasn't enough. And that false sense of security, that false sense of the safety that precaution gives, is incredibly dangerous. I wish that explosion in my hand truly taught me that lesson. I wish I had totally understood all the implications. I didn't really pay attention.

Even now, I find myself skirting to the thinnest part of the ice, walking to the very edge of the cliff. I know that I should turn back toward safety, but I choose to push the limits of the Christian envelope. I think I am strong—strong enough to handle the temptations, the images, the seducing activities. Often I am—and the firecracker explodes at the top of the arc. But just as often I am not, and the firecracker explodes, closer and with lots of pain and damage.

No one is immune to the dangers of firecrackers—or of sin. No one.

Ten

Pressure

*Your eyes saw my unformed body. All the days
ordained for me were written in your book before
one of them came to be. (Psalm 139:16)*

This is a story about a gun. My brothers and I grew
up with guns, but every time I look back on this brief
incident, a cold shudder goes through my bones. I
realize just how terrifying and complex our lives
truly are. It is not a grand recollection, but a dark
and hidden one. I never told my friends and family
about it.

The country around my hometown was very

picturesque: rolling hills, small farms, rivers, and streams. We could hike for miles through the woods or hunt for rabbits and squirrels in our backyard and beyond. We were never that far from the nearest road or house, but the woods made us feel open and free.

I grew up hunting and camping and scouting. My father and I or Tim or Bob would hunt every fall for small game such as pheasants and rabbits. And most years we hunted white-tailed deer too. I'm not sure who was responsible, but we were terrible hunters. We never shot at a deer and bagged only the occasional rabbit. But it was fun to hike the woods of the Allegheny Mountains in the clear crispness of fall.

Considering this background, it was natural that I grew up being comfortable with firearms—rifles, shotguns, pistols. I had used them all and I understood how dangerous they were. We were not manic over safety rules, but we never treated guns carelessly—until that one day in the fall of 1966.

Deep in the woods, we would target practice for hours with inexpensive .22 caliber rifles. A .22 caliber weapon is one of the smallest bore guns produced. The bullet has a diameter a bit smaller than the average pencil and is only an inch or so long. They are made for target shooting mostly; they are too small and ineffective for serious hunting. A shotgun works better on small game, and the .22 is too small for big game. However, .22s are still very dangerous. The bullet can travel more than a mile and cut through half a telephone book or virtually explode a tin can or bottle.

It was fall of my junior year of high school. There is no more beautiful spot than western Pennsylvania in the fall. The crimsons and golds and delicate reds light up the hills.

My older brother and I were over at Bruce and Dave Walthours'. About a mile from their house, down a red-shale dirt road, was a quarry . . . and local dump. It was a playground to us; bottles to throw, caves to explore, and cans to shoot at.

We all had brought our guns with us for some afternoon target practice. This was not out of the ordinary. We had done it dozens of times before. We would have competitions to determine the best marksman. And I was one of the better shooters in the group.

We probably had a couple hundred rounds between us. It was a bright and clear day. A perfect day to have fun.

We set cans up on some old timbers and proceeded to shatter the still air with the sharp coughs of our .22 rifles. Cans would fly off the boards, jagged and gaping holes torn in them. It was great fun.

We often would switch guns between us.

There is one thing you must be aware of to fully appreciate this incident. Just like every person is different, so is every gun. Two guns of exactly the same make and model will be different. They shoot differently, aim differently—and each has a different and distinctive trigger pressure. Trigger pressure is how much "pull" it takes to trip the trigger, releasing the firing mechanism, exploding the firing cap and gun powder in the shell casing, and sending the bullet spinning out of the chamber at hundreds of feet per second. Most field or hunting guns have a fairly hefty pull. In cold weather you don't want the slight pressure of a glove tripping the trigger. All I ever shot were hunting guns.

We decided to switch guns. I borrowed Bruce's pistol. It was his late father's, and it was the first time I had seen it. It was a steel blue semiautomatic pistol that had the look of a German Luger—dangerous, ominous, and cold.

I held it in my hand and gave it a heft, locked the clip, filling it with shells.

As I did this, Bruce and my brother went over to the target, set up some cans and a few bottles, and turned to walk back toward Dave and me. We were perhaps twenty-five yards away from the target. As they walked a few steps closer, I pulled up the gun into a shooting position, and as God is my witness, I have no idea why I did what I did then: I curled my finger lightly around the trigger. I knew that experienced hunters don't put their fingers on the trigger until they are ready to kill something, but there I was.

I stood there, with the pistol raised, my arm extended, my finger on the trigger.

I can see this scene as vividly today as I could twenty-five years ago.

I pulled the gun up, leveled the front sight square against Bruce's chest. I think I even gave the trigger a slight involuntary squeeze . . . and I smiled and barked out, "BANG! I GOT YOU."

Bruce calmly continued to walk toward me, and I

held the gun there until he walked out of the sights. I then took aim at an old Coke bottle, and before I even thought I touched the trigger, the gun BANGED and the bottle exploded. I went white. The trigger on this beautiful gun required no more than a breath to set it off. And there I was with a finger on that hair trigger, my friend dead in the sights, and a bullet in the chamber.

I had come within a breath of killing a friend. I am sure I would have killed him if the gun had discharged. I never said one word to anyone about this incident at the time. I pushed it from my memories, my consciousness.

Though I wasn't aware of it, this was an epiphanic moment in my life—a turning point. That breath of pressure on the trigger that day changed my life. Would it be a normal, all-American life or be forever and unalterably changed? Either I would be the kid who killed his friend or just the kid who grew up and somehow remembered this painful little incident to write about it later.

I look back and realize that that one action meant all the difference in the world. One instant, one micro-pull of pressure, one changed life. All the changes and choices in my life seem somehow tied to that one crystalline moment. Turn this way and it's easy. Turn that way and your life is bare feet on jagged glass.

Most of us know when we're about to make a big mistake. It wasn't an "accident" that I had my finger on the trigger that day.

Did God reach down and hold my trigger finger

back? I don't know if I can answer that question to anyone's satisfaction. We are creatures with free will and the ability to make horribly foolish choices. I didn't kill my friend that day, and he went on to be a Presbyterian minister.

Accidents are hard to avoid, sometimes impossible. Bad judgment, poor choices . . . well, these are things we often can control.

We all have choices in this life. Indeed, we can choose to ignore God; we can decide to turn our back on the Creator. That choice may not seem as dramatic as a loaded gun, but in the end it is the same. It is death that waits.

This incident shaped my life in thousands of subtle ways. God, through his love and protection, allowed me to experience it and come away unscathed. Looking back, I ask myself one eternally unanswerable question: "What would have happened if . . . ?" What would have happened that day if I had squeezed the trigger just one micro-ounce more? Where would my life have gone?

This incident is perhaps the biggest "what if" question of my past. It seems, in retrospect, that I have lived through many of these pivotal "what if" experiences. But in reality, there is only one "what if" question that really counts. What if I had the opportunity to receive God's gift of salvation and turned it down? What if I had life and death in my hand and chose death instead of life?

To me, that's the most frightening question.

Eleven

Fighting the Gorilla

But he said to me, "My grace is sufficient for you,
for my power is made perfect in weakness."
Therefore I will boast all the more gladly about
my weaknesses, so that Christ's power may rest
on me. (2 Corinthians 12:9)

When I was seventeen I thought I knew who the really tough guys were, who had the strength and the power to be masters of their world.

It took a gorilla to change my mind.

It was summer of 1967, a time to play softball and go on picnics. It was a time to swim and laze in the sun, a time for the age-old custom of separating suckers from their money and children from their innocence.

It was carnival time.

Picture a hot July twilight. You and your friends are cruising with a pocketful of money waiting to be spent. You park the car, and as you walk toward the lights, the noise ripples through the warm stillness— high-pitched screams from girls on the twisting Tilt-A-Whirl, the amplified shouts of the carnival barkers, the loud throbbing and thudding of 1960s rock and roll music. The Beach Boys and Jan and Dean fill the summer evening with the possibility of magic.

Then the smells meet you—so thick that they envelop you with a different color—the diesel fumes from the rides and generators, the dry, static saltiness of the popcorn, the stale grease from a million and one corn dogs and fries, the sawdust, the sweet mist of cotton candy.

One year, the carnival held by the Red Top Volunteer Fire Department in South Greensburg became the stuff of high school legend.

Summer brought out the fairs and carnivals by the dozens in western Pennsylvania. Every small hamlet, every volunteer fire department, every civic organization, every Lions club and Kiwanis group worth its salt would sponsor a carnival, or a festival, or a fair.

We were carnival connoisseurs. I was seventeen, and we had spent the previous summer going to every little town and park within a hundred-mile radius of home, attending scores of local carnivals.

Every weekend a different carnival outfit would pull into a different small town, and the weekend ritual would begin again.

Adamsburg had the best rides, and a huge outfit from Georgia brought in a dozen relatively dangerous spinning and high-velocity rides. The rides scored high in the nausea ratings. Any two rides done in quick succession preceded by a couple hot dogs and warm Cokes would tint anyone a slight green.

The best food was at Crabtree, where the ladies auxiliary of the church cooked up huge simmering vats of stuffed cabbage and sausage dripping with succulent juices. Little ladies of recent European lineage, all wearing babushkas, stood behind their tubs of food, smiling, enticing you to try one more pirogi, one more kielbasa.

The most enticing carnival was at Verona, just north of Pittsburgh, where the local officials turned a blind eye to the "attractions." The firemen set up a huge tent, filled it with blackjack tables and roulette wheels and brought a little bit of Las Vegas to the shores of the Allegheny River. Beer flowed freely at this event.

But none of them equaled the Red Top Carnival of 1967.

Every July, Sea Coast Amusements would arrive, housed in four semitrailers. Dozens and dozens of smaller trailers and step-in vans would follow, like attendants at a carnival wedding. The caravan would encircle the field, and slowly a carnival would emerge, much like a butterfly emerges from its cocoon.

The midway games would be erected first. Their canvas-and-wood frames are easy to place, like the "Penny Pitch," the "Ring around the Coke Bottle," the "Balloon Break"—all the sucker games. Food booths ring those on the outside.

At the south end of the midway were the rides. Each was framed in hundreds of light bulbs, bathed in the brightness of thousands of watts, and enveloped in the bone-rattling noise of car-sized speakers pumping out all the noise that a quality eight-track tape could offer.

But what made the 1967 Red Top Carnival truly memorable was a sideshow I have only seen once. It was there for that year alone. Whether it traveled elsewhere I do not know.

It was the sideshow that brought Chris Morris legendary status.

We sat on a grassy hillside, my friends and I, and watched the show unfold one warm summer afternoon. At the southeast end of the carnival site was a battered semitrailer, painted more white than any other color. The front of the trailer had standard metal sides and a few windows. The rear section had hinges along the top, and the panels could be folded back to the roof line. The truck headed in slowly and made its way to the far corner of the field, seeking privacy from the prying eyes of the rest of the midway. The truck stopped, the driver set his jacks under the trailer, leveled it, and drove the cab to the rear. From the rear compartment, the driver pulled out stakes and ropes and bundles and bundles of canvas sheeting.

For the next two hours, the driver hammered large metal stakes into the ground, and between the stakes he erected tall metal poles, perhaps twelve feet high, surrounding the trailer. When he was done, it looked like a postmodern, very skinny Stonehenge.

We exchanged curious glances, not knowing what to expect.

The driver, a squat, barrel-chested fellow in a torn blue T-shirt, hauled the canvas with the skill of a sailor and mounted panel after panel of it, building a fluid and gently flapping wall between the carnival and his truck.

We watched as the canvas unfurled, creaking in the gentle breeze, its wrinkles loosening and the mustiness escaping into the sunlight.

On the first panel, painted in bloodred letters, were the bold words, each letter nearly two feet tall: ARE YOU TOUGH ENOUGH TO WIN $1,000?

The question mark following the $1,000 was out of scale and in a different color—as if it had been added afterwards—perhaps the original sign painter skipped school the day they studied question marks.

The panel to the right unfurled, and painted on the canvas in gaudy glory was a twelve-foot rendition of a . . . I want to say *gorilla*, but it was more menacing, more threatening than your everyday gorilla. It was a supergorilla, emerging from the darkness of the jungle with a young, voluptuous girl carried like a rag doll in his steel-like arms. The gorilla's face was a twisted sneer, fangs and sweat and blood etched in the cruel visage. The girl was terrified into a dead faint, her hair cascading to the ground, her dress strained and tearing.

It was a truly magnificent painting. It was soul stirring. We all wanted it for our rooms. The third panel facing us unrolled with a thud. Our eyes locked on the offer presented.

Fight Kong the Killer!! Stay Upright for Sixty Seconds and Win $1,000!

Fight a gorilla? For a thousand dollars? For sixty seconds?

We stared in silence as the rest of the panels dropped, all grayed canvas with no more enticing offers, and quickly the truck—and whatever else was there—disappeared behind the wall of gray fabric.

We stared for a moment, and as we turned to each other, one name came to all in unison: "Chris Morris."

Chris Morris could have been the testosterone poster child—if there was such a thing. He was six feet four inches, blond, very muscular, very angular, and very mean.

He was the one person you never crossed. If you saw him in the hall at school and you were alone, you averted your eyes and sort of stared at the floor as you shuffled past.

It wasn't worth it to tempt the hands of fate. He would crush beer cans against his head—when they still were made of thick tin, when it still hurt to do that. He would crush the weak and the scared the same way—easily—and for the sheer pleasure of it.

If a pair of pants flew out of the boy's bathroom, you knew that Chris was terrifying a freshman. He loved confrontations. He was in it for the thrill of the battle. Owing to his size, tenacity, and brutish nature, he rarely, if ever, lost.

You win a lot, you get confident.

I know teachers were afraid of him. It was rumored that he took on a naive student teacher who pushed him a little too far in class. The words *Are you tough enough* conjured up in many minds an image of Chris. *Are you crazy enough* should have been written underneath and would have applied to Chris just as well.

Saturday night was always the high point of a carnival. The biggest crowds, the most beer, the loudest music. And Chris was going to fight the gorilla. There is no way a challenge like this could go unanswered by the toughest kid in school. We all knew that to remain champion he had to respond to the bell.

The line to see the fight stretched the entire circumference of the white canvas fence. For five dollars we could watch the fight of the century. The audience was packed with fellow students and the curious. It would be a good purse tonight.

The sides of the rear of the trailer were folded up. Built into the truck was a "ring of steel." Heavy, black steel bars were the frame of the trailer, creating a metal cage about twenty-five feet long and twelve feet wide. The floor was covered in a thick carpet of fresh straw.

The master of ceremonies, the owner, the driver, the roustabout, the ringmaster, the trainer came out from a small door in the front of the trailer. They were all one in the same squat little man.

He wore a shiny black satin jacket. Stitched in the fabric, over his heart, was a single word: ACE. Embroidered across the back was a magnificent eagle, holding a snake in its talons. Around his neck he placed a microphone attached to a coat-hanger frame, padded with coils and coils of medical tape. The tape was yellowed and frayed.

He welcomed us to the most unique sideshow any man ever devised.

"And now, ladies and gentlemen, this is the moment you have been dreaming about. Who will be the king of the jungle? Who will be the new champion?" The crowd was shouting and clapping. "Let me introduce you to the challenger, Chris Morris."

Chris jumped to the top step outside the trailer, below the entrance door. The crowd cheered wildly. He looked a little stunned by the ovation, or perhaps a little stunned by the two six-packs of Iron City that he had drunk that afternoon, building up courage for the evening. He was clearly encouraged by the cheers and proceeded to beat on his chest, gorilla style, as the crowd hooted and cheered.

"And now, ladies and gentlemen, allow me to introduce the champion of the world, the undisputed master of the jungle and the king of the beasts. . . . " The words hung out in the air as he waited. The audience held its breath as one. "Here is Kong . . . the mighty, the awesome, the magnificent Kong!" And he reached behind the door and pulled on the heaviest and thickest stainless steel chain I had ever seen, and Kong slowly, methodically, carefully lumbered out into the ring.

He was not just a gorilla—he was a huge gorilla. As tall as he was wide, the animal filled up five cubic feet of solid gorilla space. He slowly walked toward his trainer, the ringmaster. A wide leather strap was around Kong's neck, maybe three inches wide and thick, decorated with studs and rhinestones. A muzzle was on his mouth to prevent him from using his teeth and fangs.

He was immense. It seemed as if his arms were as thick as a telephone pole, and sculpted muscles rippled beneath his fur.

I glanced over at Chris. The color had gone out of his face.

"Kong, come here," the ringmaster shouted. The huge beast ambled over. The trainer gave him a steel bar, thicker than my thumb. Kong took it in his two hands and stared back at the crowd. The bar began to bend, slowly at first, and in a moment, it was a U-shaped piece of steel. He had done it without straining, without batting a gorilla eyelash.

Chris looked even whiter.

The gorilla looked over at Chris, and for a moment I saw the sadness in the animal's eyes. He looked like a punch-drunk fighter, one rung from the bottom of the ladder, doing a whistle-stop tour of penny-ante towns for the last time.

He walked toward the door, and Chris took his first step backwards. We all knew that the gorilla would be able to literally kill anyone in a matter of seconds.

The owner was an old pro. A few steps before the door he called out, "Kong, wait."

Kong stopped and looked over his shoulder to the voice.

"He's pretty small for you, isn't he?"

In a practiced way, Kong nodded his head slowly.

"Want to take a break tonight?"

Kong nodded again, on cue.

"OK, Kong, why don't you take it easy, and we'll get your cousin to finish tonight."

Kong looked relieved and picked up his chain and walked back through the door, turning sideways to fit in.

Some of the color had returned to Chris's face.

A few seconds later, the owner came back out with a monkey—about the size of the average family dog. Not a very intimidating creature.

"All right, Chris, let's get in the ring and meet Kong's little cousin—Baby Kong!"

Chris was going to fight this little rag. He would win in a second. How hard would it be to corral a small monkey? Chris was smiling again. I think I saw his eyes start to count his $1,000 prize.

Chris bounded up the steps and leapt through the open cage door and into the ring, lightly dancing on the toes of his feet, weaving and bobbing and throwing punches.

Baby Kong was muzzled as well and was lazily swinging from a bar in the ceiling, holding on with a one-armed nonchalance. If you looked closely, you could see Baby Kong's eyes—mean and dark. They were the eyes of a fighter who enjoyed the work.

"Baby Kong, are you ready?" the ringmaster shouted.

Baby Kong nodded vigorously.

"Chris, are you ready?"

Chris pounded on his chest again in an act of bravado to affirm his readiness to do battle.

"No biting, no choking, no foreign objects," the ringmaster cried, explaining all the rules that were necessary. "If you pin Baby Kong in sixty seconds, a thousand bucks is yours."

"Ready. Set. Go!"

And with that Chris charged at Baby Kong. With a deft jump, Baby Kong hit the floor, bounced sideways, and grabbed at Chris's shirt. In a flurry, his shirt was in tatters around his neck.

Another lunge and the monkey ricocheted off the bars and went feet first at Chris's nose, then swung around on his back and jabbed and clawed at his ears and hair, all the time screeching at the top of his lungs. Chris was shouting loudly, almost frantically, "Hold still you stupid monkey!"

After about thirty seconds of this loud, frenzied mayhem, the straw in the cage was spread into the corners and dust filled the air, dancing and sparkling in the spotlights. Chris was in one corner, gasping for breath, his shirt torn to shreds, his hair wild, scratches on his face and back, his nose bloodied. Perhaps it would have been a good time to warn him of the bad effects of smoking two packs of Marlboros a day.

Baby Kong held on to a bar in the ceiling and swung back and forth . . . slowly . . . methodically . . . maliciously.

Yes, it would have been a terrible life for these two

animals. I am sure that today the ASPCA would shut it down in a second. But at least Baby Kong had the immense pleasure of beating the stuffing out of every two-bit bully in every two-bit town between Maine and Florida. I swear I saw Baby Kong smile as he let go of the bar. He bounded onto the floor and with the speed of Muhammad Ali went feet first into Chris's nose again.

A vacant look appeared in Chris's eyes as his knees got wobbly and he teetered back and forth—and then with a thud, went bottom first into the straw. Baby Kong jumped back to his perch, then back into the arms of the ringmaster as the sixty-second bell sounded.

The audience was subdued as we filed out of the show. A couple of Chris's friends helped him to his feet and steered him through the crowds that parted on both sides of the injured warrior like the wake of a boat. Chris's eyes remained unfocused for several days. In the future, many whispered voices would recall the time that Chris was beaten bloody by a little pet monkey. The whispers would be there, as a quiet and hushed afterthought, just as Chris passed from hearing range.

Such a big person and such a little animal. Maybe Chris couldn't beat up a monkey. Maybe nobody could.

It was funny, but the foundations of my high school beliefs started to tremble that night, and large cracks appeared. It was one of the first times my perception of my world suddenly shifted and realigned.

If Chris wasn't the boss, who was? Apparently he wasn't the tough guy I thought he was. And where did that put me? Where was my rung on the ladder of power and status?

Chris was no match for a fifty-pound primate with an attitude.

Chris wasn't the only person fighting a bigger or stronger opponent. Years earlier, I thought I could lick the world all by myself, could live my life as I saw fit, handling whatever fight life had to offer. I could use my wits and my intellect and win any battle.

And you know, like Chris, I won a few of those battles on my own. At least I think they were on my own. And so I got cocky. I was reckless, and I tempted fate a few times too many.

The problem with doing battle on your own is that you get used to it. Even when you start losing, you know no other way to handle your problems. Sometime before my twenty-fifth high school reunion, I heard that Chris was the same as ever, still getting into fights at the local VFW, still seeking out those who were weaker, still asserting his dominance. But the sad part is that Chris is no longer the terror of high school. Too much drinking, too much smoking, too many fights, too many pounds around his middle—all have taken their toll. Often as not, he is now on the losing end. The years add up as the reflexes slow down.

I see Chris today and know that is what would have happened to me had I continued to fight with the world—fighting God, really—trying to see who was really in control of things. I finally realized just who the King was in my life. It didn't take a physical fight, but a mental one. I am very glad that God allowed Kong the gorilla and his little monkey cousin to fight someone else to help point me to the truth.

Twelve

The Green Hornet and the Meaning of Life

Do not store up for yourselves treasures on earth, where moth and rust destroy, and where thieves break in and steal. But store up for yourselves treasures in heaven, where moth and rust do not destroy, and where thieves do not break in and steal. For where your treasure is, there your heart will be also. (Matthew 6:19-21)

Imagine, if you will, thousands of parts, milled to exacting tolerances, carefully designed and engineered, nesting within a pool of other parts, functioning in perfect harmony. Each piece, from the tiniest bolt to pieces the size of the average sofa, is geared and woven together with the others to produce one of the marvels of modern technology: the automobile.

Indeed, each singular vehicle is a feat of man's engineering genius, his proclivity to masterful inventiveness. The car is one of the pinnacles of the industrial revolution.

With the exception of one car—a green 1955 Plymouth four-door coupe. We called it the Green Hornet.

The year was 1967. I was seventeen years old with a driver's license. A teenager with a license is cool—too cool to ride a bike. We were also too cool for the family car—either big beige sedans or boatlike station wagons. We needed transportation that fit our image. And image is critical to seventeen-year-olds.

If desire were dollars, we would all have been driving Porsches that summer.

As a group, Bill, Eddie, Pez, and myself were miserable. No one had cool wheels. Our family cars would do in an emergency, but only just barely. Complicating matters, our turf was geographically immense, spreading from Irwin in the west to Latrobe in the east, and required a tankful of gas to reconnoiter every possible pool hall, fast food restaurant, and hangout. Doing the tour in the family car would involve dying a slow death of embarrassment.

The solution to our transportation problem came to us in a flash. Actually, it was a real flash. Bill was driving his father's Olds 88, trying to see just how fast we could make it from the Eat 'n' Park in Jean-

nette to Winky's hamburger stand south of the valve
plant. Our parents' cars were well suited for some
activities after all.

As we sped past the Boron station in Lincoln
Heights, one of the passengers, straining to stay
upright, peered at the lot behind the garage. Nestled
among the Queen Anne's lace and thistles was a car.
Not just any car, but one with dark and ominous
lines, a rakish look, the look of speed, the look of a
car that perhaps we might be able to afford. Spelled
out across the windshield, in huge white letters, were
two tantalizing words: For Sale.

We skidded back to the lot, fishtailing across
the cement apron, and in a furious rush, converged
on the old car. We peered in the windows, we ran
our hands over the fenders, we kicked the tires.
Cars had been bought and sold for decades before
we stumbled onto this particular car, but it was
as if our group's collective consciousness of the
process clicked together at the same time. No one
wanted to be the first to suggest anything. We
circled the car several times. We stroked our chins
thoughtfully.

An old man in a gray uniform strolled out from
the station. He knew he had a nibble on the line and
wanted to play the fish just right so as not to lose
his catch.

"Nice car, ain't she?"

A beauty, we all agreed, obviously overlooking the
rust at the bottom of the doors, the cracked back
window, the very bald tires, the faded paint of the
old car. The list went on and on.

"A 1955 Plymouth," he added proudly. "They don't make 'em that way anymore."

"With good reason," we should have said. But the nectar of owning our own new car tasted sweet, and we stayed silent.

"You boys interested in buying it?" he asked.

Well, we don't know, we might be, it all depends, and could you tell us something about the car? Are there any problems? We tried to remember what our fathers had said at car showrooms and how they had acted. It was different now that we were asking the questions.

A little old lady had just finished driving it, he said, although it was a real cream puff. It had lots of life left in it. "You'll kick yourself if you let this one get away. Another guy wants to buy it, but he won't have the money till payday."

Money . . . we hadn't thought about that.

"I'd suggest buying it now 'cause I can't guarantee it's going to be here long."

Money . . . we hadn't thought about that at all.

We exchanged unknowing glances. One of us asked, "How much?"

The old man looked at us, looked down at his feet, looked back at the station, then said. "Tell you what, boys. I like you. And because I like you, I'll let you have it for even less than the other fellow was offering. That sound fair?"

We agreed that it did, but we hadn't heard any figures yet.

He rubbed the stubble of his greasy chin. "I hate to do this 'cause I know I could do better, but, what the heck. I'll let you have it for . . ." He paused as he did calculations in his head. "I'll let you have it for two hundred bucks even."

Everyone thought of the same number at the same time: fifty dollars.

We could each chip in a quarter of the total cost, have the car a quarter of the time and, since we were always together, we would be using it all the time.

Fifty dollars. Each of us could manage that.

A mere fifty dollars and we could have our own set of wheels, or at least a quarter of the wheels. Each of us would literally own a wheel of our own.

The next day, with fifty dollars in each of four hands, we headed over to the station. Cash was placed on the barrelhead, and the car was ours.

I made us stop at the K mart between the station and Bill's home, where the car was to be stored for the first week.

The seats of a well-used car were very well used, and tufts of white padding kept escaping from the numerous cuts and tears, floating in the breezes of the open windows. It would not do for our car. Twelve dollars and ninety-five cents later, we were installing new seat covers in the parking lot of K mart. We selected the dark green covers, but for the seat bottoms only because the seat backs had far fewer tears. The colors of the covers and the seats matched—if you sort of squinted at it—from a distance. The car was cleaner now, and definitely newer looking.

We also got one of those little pine-soaked trees and hung it from the rearview mirror.

And it smelled new.

Those first few weeks the car ran well; a slight

whine going up hills, a bit of smoke, and a few lurches. And you had to pump the brakes to get it to stop, but that was OK. We still stopped eventually.

We christened it "The Green Hornet." It had a few quirks. Nine days after taking possession of the Green Hornet we encountered our first major problem—in reality, the only major problem with the car.

Pez noticed it first. The car was becoming reluctant to slip into reverse. A gentle tug on the gear selector was all that was required at first, then ever-increasing arm pressure, until, on that ninth day, the driver had to ask for assistance from the passenger. We did not think that was normal.

We drove it back to the Boron station and asked to speak to Gus, our auto salesman. We were informed that he hadn't shown up for a couple of days and no one was sure if he was ever coming back. But, we explained, we have this problem with the car he sold us. It wouldn't go into reverse.

The current old man in gray overalls peered out at the car and smiled. "I can fix that in a jiffy. Bring her into the bay."

In a moment, the Green Hornet was perched up on the hoist, its rusting underbelly exposed to our peering eyes. What delicate adjustment was needed, we wondered. What complicated tooling was required to fix our precious vehicle?

The new Gus walked over to a greasy corner of the shop, rummaged through some long-handled tools, and walked back to us carrying . . . a sledgehammer. He hefted it to his shoulder, took careful aim, and with a roundhouse overhead swing, whacked the bottom of the transmission housing with all his might. We stared, wide-eyed, as the bang reverberated among the used tires and oil cans. Rust sprinkled down from various parts of the chassis.

"There ya go," the new Gus said as he lowered the car to the floor. "That'll be a dollar."

That was it? The new Gus explained, "Sometimes the gearing and the trannies on these old cars need to be loosened a bit." A sledge was the best way to get their attention, he added, advising that we carry one at all times—just in case.

The car worked like a dream—for another fourteen hours till it froze in neutral. We had packed Bill's father's five-pound mini sledgehammer, and I crawled underneath the car in the parking lot of the Mount Odin golf course and whacked away a few times near the spot on the transmission that the new Gus had whacked at.

It worked, and the gearshift slid easily into first gear.

We marveled at our newfound ability to work on cars.

However, this process complicated many other processes. Like going on dates. One of us was designated as "the hammer," and we carried an old throw rug for rainy or muddy conditions. But crawling underneath a car was not a pleasant experience, regardless of the preparations we took, and our dates were never quite as impressed as we were. Sitting in the backseat of a decaying old car, with the guy you were dating underneath it, hammering away, making the entire car vibrate and tremble, just to find first gear, was not a way to impress anyone.

The Green Hornet lasted for five weeks after the first sledging. In the parking lot behind the Youngwood pool hall, the car stopped, and no amount of hammering could dislodge the gears.

We all had hope of a cure until Pez took a mighty six-inch swing, banged on the housing, and the head of the sledge disappeared into the transmission. Nasty oil mixed with gear shavings and metal bits covered the hammer. This was a "broken" that a sledgehammer could never fix. We knew that a new transmission would cost more than the entire car—a lot more.

We used three long leather belts to secure the front bumper of the Hornet to the back bumper of Greg's red Studebaker and hauled it three miles down the road to the scrapyard on Route 119.

We got ten dollars for the car, which we split five ways, paying Greg two dollars for his towing.

I learned two very important lessons that summer. Lessons that I have remembered and that have taught me a little more about how God views things.

The first and perhaps most important lesson is finding out that nothing will last forever. Especially 1955 Plymouths. Very few material things are as good as they seem. Everything we own, no matter how excited we are about owning it, will eventually disappoint us. The four of us loved that car—for a few days—and as it rolled into the junkyard that day, we all felt more than a little betrayed.

The Bible talks about how the treasures that we store up on earth will tarnish, discolor, rust, and decay. We experienced each one of those conditions during that summer. And that has stayed with me. I truly enjoy the new things I buy and use, but I realize that such joy is fleeting at best and that all too soon the shiny new—whatever—will be bent, rusted, and discarded. How much more wise it is to store up heavenly treasures, like friendship, like love, like serving others—things that God will honor.

There was a second of life's important lessons I learned from that old Plymouth. Sometimes you have to get dirty to get things to work. Everything good comes with a price, and sometimes that price includes getting dirty to get it done. Christians sometimes hesitate to plunge into life because it will alter and muss up their vision of the "proper, neat, and tidy" world. But getting dirty, getting covered with life, is often what it takes to get things moving forward.

I realize that making a spiritual application from hammering on a frozen transmission with a sledgehammer is a bit of a stretch, but it is true. Twenty-seven years ago I realized that making progress often required getting into some uncomfortable situations. And you know what? It still does.

Thirteen

New Year's Eve

*Joy and gladness are gone from the orchards and
fields of Moab. I have stopped the flow of wine
from the presses; no one treads them with shouts
of joy. Although there are shouts, they are not
shouts of joy. (Jeremiah 48:33)*

It was New Year's Eve in western Pennsylvania. A
time to celebrate and sing about old acquaintances
and friends. A time to have the best time of the year.
The year was 1972 and I was just twenty-two. Looking back through that era of my life, it feels like I'm
looking at a different person—someone who lived

in a different world. That New Year's evening, I stopped and picked up my friends, Greg and Jimmy. We were the quintessential "rebels without a cause." We were wild and crazy, dangerous and volatile. None of us had a steady girlfriend. At the time we just couldn't figure why. In retrospect, the reasons are pretty apparent.

No one we knew was holding a New Year's Eve party. We were home from college, and most of our high school friends had drifted away. Our pool of party contacts was pretty shallow this year. But we were optimistic. We planned to go to our favorite tavern for the evening, sit and watch the festivities on television, play some darts, have a few brewskies. That's what we planned.

We stopped at The Point, a small bar located in a wedge-shaped building—hence the name—and sidled up to the bar. No sooner had we bought our first round when Bob the Bartender called loudly, "LAST CALL!"

"What?!" we cried. "We just got here. It's only 8:00!"

"Look around," Bob said.

We did and discovered that the bar, other than us and one other die-hard patron, was empty. It did seem a little odd.

"Everyone is at parties," Bob explained, "or at fancy restaurants with a band and a real celebration and a cover charge, and of course you guys would need dates. So I can see why you're here."

Oh.

We grumbled, got our coats, vowing that there are

other places that would welcome a few lost souls on that cold night.

At our second choice—Mr. Toad's—the owner was locking the door as we drove up.

"Don't you have a party to go to?" he yelled. "Everybody else does."

Talk about your holiday cheer!

We drove to our third choice. It was closed. Our fourth choice was closed. Our really desperate fifth choice was open for another fifteen minutes.

I hope I don't offend readers who see drinking as an unpardonable and terrible sin. Going to bars and drinking was the only lifestyle we knew. It was accepted. None of us felt abnormal. None of us felt the least bit doomed.

At that last, truly desperate choice of taverns, the owner snapped off the lights, and we picked up a couple of six-packs and spent the next three or four hours driving through the towns and neighborhoods where we had grown up and gone to school. We sipped the beer, hiding the cans as cars came into view, feeling more and more lost and lonely.

I was home before midnight that year, before the celebrations and the cheers and Dick Clark and Times Square.

All we wanted was a warm place to let us in. All we wanted was someone to be with. All we wanted was someone to talk to—besides each other, of course. Even if it was only for a few hours.

We didn't find it that year.

It's a terrible feeling—being all alone, as if you didn't belong. Our trouble was that we had been away too long, had lost all our old contacts and friends, people who might have invited us to their parties.

Sometimes it's other things that keep us feeling apart, lonely, separated from friends. There's a story in the Bible from the Gospel of John about a woman who, for a number of reasons, felt left out.

Jesus had been in Jerusalem and was on his way back to Galilee. He chose to go through Samaria, a route most other Jews wouldn't take because they didn't like the Samaritans very much—especially *sinful* Samaritans. Around noon, as Jesus and his disciples approached the village of Sychar, he came to Jacob's well, located on the parcel of ground Jacob gave to his son Joseph. John tells the story:

> Jesus was tired from the long walk in the hot sun and sat wearily beside the well.
>
> Soon a Samaritan woman came to draw water, and Jesus asked her for a drink. He was alone at the time as his disciples had gone into the village to buy some food. The woman was surprised that a Jew would ask a "despised Samaritan" for anything—usually they wouldn't even speak to them!—and she remarked about this to Jesus.
>
> He replied, "If you only knew what a wonderful gift God has for you, and who I am, you would ask me for some *living* water!"
>
> "But you don't have a rope or a bucket," she said, "and this is a very deep

well! Where would you get this living water?
And besides, are you greater than our ances-
tor Jacob? How can you offer better water
than this which he and his sons and cattle
enjoyed?"

Jesus replied that people soon became
thirsty again after drinking this water. "But
the water I give them," he said, "becomes a
perpetual spring within them, watering them
forever with eternal life."

"Please, sir," the woman said, "give
me some of that water! Then I'll never be
thirsty again and won't have to make this
long trip out here every day."

"Go and get your husband," Jesus told her.

"But I'm not married," the woman
replied.

"All too true!" Jesus said. "For you
have had five husbands, and you aren't even
married to the man you're living with now."

"Sir," the woman said, "you must be a
prophet. But say, tell me, why is it that you
Jews insist that Jerusalem is the only place of
worship, while we Samaritans claim it is here
[at Mount Gerizim], where our ancestors
worshiped?"

Jesus replied, "The time is coming,
ma'am, when we will no longer be concerned
about whether to worship the Father here or
in Jerusalem. For it's not *where* we worship
that counts, but *how* we worship—is our
worship spiritual and real? Do we have the

109

Holy Spirit's help? For God is Spirit, and we must have his help to worship as we should. The Father wants this kind of worship from us. But you Samaritans know so little about him, worshiping blindly, while we Jews know all about him, for salvation comes to the world through the Jews."

The woman said, "Well, at least I know that the Messiah will come—the one they call Christ—and when he does, he will explain everything to us."

Then Jesus told her, "I am the Messiah!" (John 4:2-26, TLB)

Interesting, isn't it, how long some people have been searching for a place to belong and someone to make them feel as if they belong. Some have been on the quest for a long, long time.

That New Year's Eve came and went, and it left us lonely and adrift. There was no place in the world that cold evening that would provide us a safe harbor, a warm hearth, a listening soul. It took me another eight years to find someone who would satisfy the longings I felt that night.

Eight more years was a long time to be left searching, a long time to be without a home. The problem was that I, like this Samaritan woman, had been looking to the wrong places and the wrong people— even drinking from the wrong wells. But that day she found the right place and the right Person to give her the drink that really satisfied. I'm glad she found him—and I'm glad I did too.

Fourteen

The Hitchhiker

In reply Jesus said: "A man was going down from Jerusalem to Jericho, when he fell into the hands of robbers. They stripped him of his clothes, beat him and went away, leaving him half dead. A priest happened to be going down the same road, and when he saw the man, he passed by on the other side. So too, a Levite, when he came to the place and saw him, passed by on the other side. But a Samaritan, as he traveled, came where the man was; and when he saw him, he took pity on him. He went to him and bandaged his wounds, pouring on oil and wine. Then he put

*the man on his own donkey, took him to an inn
and took care of him. The next day he took out
two silver coins and gave them to the innkeeper.
'Look after him,' he said, 'and when I return, I will
reimburse you for any extra expense you may
have.'"* (Luke 10:30-35)

Every generation sees its own age group as the last
of the innocents. I grew up in a generation that sang
about "peace, love, and understanding." It wasn't
innocent, but when viewing the past, distance dilutes
the dangers. My coming-of-age era was a time when
an adventurous youth could hitchhike across country, or back and forth to school. Not every passing
car held a mass murderer or sexual deviant. In the
sixties, it seemed that fewer people were filled with
homicidal rages.

Things were . . . groovy.

(Did anyone else wince when reading that word
groovy? How easy it was to say it twenty years ago
and honestly mean it!)

If you looked at some of my pictures from back
then—or at the photos of my friends—you would
insist that no one would ever have picked us up as
we hitched rides. Never. Never in a million years.
Not even a homicidal maniac would have seen us as
suitable traveling companions. Why? We were fully
decked out in the style of the hippie generation.

(*Hippie* is another word that makes me wince
when I have to say it. How easy it was back then to
describe yourself as a hippie—and think it was . . .
groovy!)

We wore our hair long and flowing. We had beards. Our clothes, as well, had the well-worn grunge look—Goodwill-store clothes, patched blue jeans, purposefully frayed at the cuffs, bell-bottoms, beads, tie-dyed everything, sandals, and headbands.

My generation saw hitchhiking as a liberating method of transport. One fewer pollution-spewing vehicle crowding the highways. One fewer person using up earth's finite resources. Of course, it is much easier to stand in strident opposition to the internal combustion engine when you can't afford to buy one.

Hitchhiking was a capricious mode of travel, like a dandelion puff in the wind. It could take all day to travel a hundred miles if the rides didn't come. It could take you seventy-eight minutes to travel a hundred miles if you were picked up by a black Corvette with a radar detector on a lonely four-lane highway, driven by a good old boy chain-smoking Salems and chugging from a thermos of coffee, often steering with his knees. (That's my hitchhiking land speed record.)

Our routes would not always be straight and to the point, but zigging and zagging. One traveled with the vagaries of random selection. Farther along the road was always better, even if the rides angled north and south of your destination. To misquote Thomas Wolfe, one could always go home; it just took longer some days than others.

A short ten-minute ride down the road required a smile and an outstretched arm. A longer ride, more than an hour, entailed preparation. The required equipment: a square piece of cardboard, a black Magic Marker to boldly outline your traveling goals: New York City, Pittsburgh, State College. A more adventuresome traveler might illustrate his traveling goals with a single word: East, West, South, or North.

Once, as I hitched a ride in the backseat of a powder blue Cadillac, we passed a young girl hitchhiking. Her life story was summed up in a single, plaintive word written in blue Magic Marker two feet high. All her sign said was PLEASE. It looked well used. You would see signs written in pencil that no one could read, or signs with incredible destinations written on them: ALASKA seen in the back roads of Georgia, or CALIFORNIA seen in the Allegheny mountains. In my opinion, that was too big a trip to get your hands on. Most drivers wanted no part of a crusade. They just wanted some company for an hour or two.

Let's relax and think back to those groovy days, when we were free from the confines of an outdated culture.

It is October of 1969. I am nineteen years old, a recent high school graduate.

Juniata College was the school I planned to attend. It was the only one I applied to. Why? Well, it was the school my older brother attended—and the school he got kicked out of for sneaking a beer into his room. I chose it out of inertia, I suppose.

Juniata was nestled in the Allegheny Mountains and was a two-and-a-half hour drive from our home. From our house, you took Route 66 north to Delmont, then onto Route 22 through Blairsville, and on through

Clyde, then Armagh and Dilltown, then NantyGlo and Ebensburg, then Munster and past Gallitzin, through Summit past Tunnel Hill, passing just south of Altoona, through Hollidaysburg, past Canoe Creek to Water Street. At Water Street you faced a T in the road. Stay on Route 22 south for a long, lonely, desolate stretch of road and you would find yourself in Huntingdon, the home of Juniata College.

If you turned north at Water Street, headed past Union Furnace, past Tyrone, past Bald Eagle, then Hannah, Port Matilda, Buffalo Run, and Waddle, you came to State College and Penn State University—where most of my friends planned to attend, along with 25,000 other students.

Huntingdon, a town of 7,000, might be charitably called picturesque. It was small, isolated, and depressing. I visited the biggest store in town, a department store of some local note, asking for the most recent Beatles record. "Oh yes, I think we have that ordered and we should have it in a month or two. Do you want it in mono or stereo?"

I had to drive fifty miles to find a Ping-Pong paddle to replace the one I broke. We had few diversions. The best restaurant in town was a truck stop on the highway. However they did make great cherry pie.

As a freshman, one was required to live on campus, and cars were not allowed. But being the last in a family of five meant living with hand-me-downs, which I thought was a barbaric practice, until my older brothers started to leave both the family homestead as well as their cars behind. I had unlimited

access to several cars as a junior and senior in high
school. It was a freedom that I wanted to keep.

I surreptitiously failed to register the car that I
brought with me that first week of school. I parked it
in a different lot every night so as to arouse no suspicion. I collected a few quasi-tickets, discarding them
with disdain. Eventually, the dean of students cor-
nered me. In stern, staccato terms, he instructed me
to get the car out of there and back home.

Imagining the prospects of a tragically diminished
social life without wheels, I sadly drove my car
home, where a second plan germinated. A car was
big, a motorcycle was smaller. A car is easy to spot,
hard to hide. A motorcycle was hard to spot and
easy to hide—in the bushes, behind the Dumpster, in
the basement of the dorm. So I rode my motorcycle
back to school. And the bike allowed at least two of
us to get cherry pie at 3 A.M.

But it was too late. I was being monitored. I soon
faced another meeting with the dean of students.
And the motorcycle had to go.

It was early November, and three hours on a
motorcycle in forty-degree weather is downright
uncomfortable.

Early Friday morning, the first weekend of
November, I walked the two miles to Route 22,
held out my very colorful sign with Greensburg
written on it, and headed home. (Few people in
Pennsylvania, even, have heard of Jeannette.) A
couple of hours later and I was home, in my faithful VW beetle, and on my way back to Juniata.
Early the following morning, I retrieved my bike

from the bushes, removed the front wheel, tied the axle to the rear bumper with several hundred feet of clothesline, and headed back home for a second time that weekend.

My older brother Tim was home on a week's leave from the army. He offered to take me back to school. We set off early Sunday morning.

That Sunday was one of those rare fall days where the sky is so blue and clear that you can see past the sun, almost into space and to the very stars themselves. The air was chilled, clean, and crisp. It was a perfect day for a drive through the mountains, and we cut through the early morning mists in the hollows, barreling up the steep grades of the Alleghenies.

On our route, one would often pass by hitchhikers on their way back to Penn State. If we had room we stopped. But the roads were empty; most students wouldn't be on the roads until after lunch.

Driving through Hollidaysburg on this cold, still, Sunday morning, we passed a more unusual site. He was a black man in his late twenties with his thumb out and a desperate, cold look on his face. He carried no luggage.

We slowed to the side of the road and opened the door, shoving duffel bags and empty cans to the side. He sprinted up, crawled in the backseat, and we were off.

He had a light summer jacket on, not geared to early winter. It was clearly road worn.

We made small talk. "How you doing?" "Cold out there?" "Where you heading?"

"New York City," he replied.

"New York? That's a long way off, and this isn't a very direct route."

"Well, I sort of jumped a freight train in Minneapolis to get there and this hick sheriff sort of caught me and I spent last night in jail. He drove me over to that road this morning and said 'I want you out of town. Now.' So now I'm on my way."

"Minneapolis? That's where our brother lives," we said.

"Yeh, where's he hang out?" he asked.

Hang out? We didn't know. We had only visited there once, and my brother wasn't the type to hang out anywhere, but I mentioned the name of a sort of restaurant and bar that we passed once on the way to his apartment.

"The Lincoln Inn," I said.

"Oh yeh, that's where I hang out," he quickly replied. "Is your brother a tall guy?"

An easy guess, since both Tim and I are more than six feet tall.

"Yeh."

"Skinny guy?"

"Yeh."

"What's his name?" he asked.

"Bob. His friends call him Red."

"Oh yeh, I know him. Red and me, he's all right. We hang out there together," he said.

Tim and I shot sidelong glances at each other, knowing full well that this guy had never met our brother, but it was groovy that he thought he knew him and he rambled on for a while about what he and Bob did back in Minneapolis.

Looking back, I now realize that he wanted to connect, somehow, to someone that could offer comfort, security, even if only for a moment.

I asked, "Where you going in New York? You have family there?"

"Nah," he answered, "but there are a lot of brothers there."

Well, yes, that was true. Did he know any of them, I wondered, but did not ask.

In a few more minutes, we had come to Water Street and the T in the road. We stopped the car and pulled off to the side.

I turned to face our rider in the rear seat and said, "If you go north to Penn State on this road, the rides would be much better. There's not much traffic heading south. If you follow Route 220—that heads pretty much east into New York City. I don't think you'll stand as good of a chance to make it to New York if we take you with us to Huntingdon. It would take you a lot longer if you stay with us."

He looked a bit apprehensive, maybe a bit scared as he looked at the barren roadside where he would be getting out. No homes, no businesses, no one around.

He pointed north and asked, "Go up that road?"

"Yeh," I said. "About thirty miles or so and you'll hit Penn State."

"Penn State," he repeated, perhaps never having heard of it before.

"Thirty miles."

"Yep."

"The rides will be better heading north," I said trying to assure him.

"You sure?"

"Yep." And his trip would be easier on that route.
It really would be. But a small part of me also
wanted him gone. I didn't want to have to worry
about his troubles. I had troubles of my own.

He slowly crawled out of the car, looked about for
a moment as if to get his bearings, carefully shut the
car door, and began to walk to the east side of the
road.

"Good luck," I called through my rolled-down
window.

"Thanks, man. Thanks for the ride."

He bunched the collar of his jacket around his
neck, and my brother put the car in gear and got
back on the highway to Huntingdon.

I'm sure he was broke. I'm sure that he knew no
one in New York City. I'm sure he had no place to
stay when he got there. I turned and looked as we
drove off, and I saw him shrink in the distance. After
a moment or two, after a mile or two, I turned to
Tim and said, "We should have given the guy twenty
bucks or something."

Tim paused and said, "Yeh, we should have."

He was poor and broke and black and lost in the
middle of the Allegheny Mountains on a cold Sunday
in November. To this day, this is the image I see
when I think of being desperate or lonely or helpless
or alone.

I don't know why he came to be there. Maybe he
was in trouble with the law. Maybe he had used up
all his chances in Minneapolis. Maybe he was trying
to make a new start. All I really know for sure is that

I didn't really help him get to where he was going—other than a few miles in my car.

I didn't know Jesus then and I would have never asked myself that old question "What would Jesus have done?" I wish I had, though. What would I have done? What could I have done? Given him money, bought him lunch, driven him to the turnpike an hour's drive south, put him up in a cheap motel for the night—there were dozens of ways I could have helped a fellowman.

But I did none of those things. I drove away . . . clean.

I could have made a difference in his life. I could have made an impact. I could have shown Christian love.

Life is full of these over-the-shoulder glances into the past. I wish I had known who Jesus was that day. I pray that I would have done something different. Something more. Something that Jesus would have done.

Fifteen

The Water Buffalo and the Opel

Do not oppress an alien; you yourselves know how
it feels to be aliens, because you were aliens in
Egypt. (Exodus 23:9)

I have a habit of noticing people as they first enter
a room—whether it is at a restaurant, an office,
or a church. I can always spot a first-timer; their
eyes give them away. There is an unsettled look,
an almost fearful air about them. Their eyes open
wide and dart from left to right, trying to see everything quickly in a rush to acclimate themselves
to the new surroundings. A large room, full of

strange people, is an intimidating prospect for many.

I know—I have felt that fear that comes with crossing a strange threshold. And this story is about two water buffalo who have experienced it as well.

The year was 1972. I was twenty-two years old. My brother Tim, our parents, and I had embarked on a seven-week tour of Europe. It was a tour of odd proportions, odd highlights, odd memories.

The plane trip, from Cleveland, Ohio, to Frankfurt, Germany, was chartered by the Ohio Transylvanian Saxon group. It provided an inexpensive method to get to Europe. My father had wanted to go back to the "old country" his entire life. It had been more than five decades, more than a half-century, since he had seen vistas from his childhood, stories about which he had told and retold during those fifty years. Despite his lifetime in America, the "Heimatland" or homeland was calling out to his soul, beckoning him to rejoin his past. Melodies from the old Saxon songs echoed faintly inside his heart.

Dad wanted to visit Romania to see his aging Uncle John, his father's brother. Romania and Uncle John lay many days' journey east of Frankfurt. From the moment we touched down we relentlessly made our way toward that goal. On the way, we traversed the southern Alps, we experienced Vienna, we enjoyed a cruise along the Rhine. But my father, without saying it, kept looking east and kept us pointed toward his ancestral and spiritual home.

My brother joked that when we left Austria for Hungary, we went from color scenery to scenery in black and white. If Hungary was black and white, Romania was at that time even worse—smaller, darker, and broodingly depressing.

Romania was a secretive, suspicious country, and the uniformed and heavily armed border guards were exactingly deliberate in their search of our car. They kept glancing back at us as they rummaged through our belongings. I imagine they wondered why anyone would visit Romania. They carefully examined our family photo album, looking for classified pictures, pointing at the shots that showed our home and family.

In Hermanstadt (now Sibiu), the capital city of my father's childhood Transylvania, we arrived at the only hotel in the small city. As we climbed the front steps, we were stopped by a small man in an ill-fitting suit. In broken English, German, and Romanian, he offered us a bargain. Rather than stay at the government-run hotel at probably one hundred dollars per person per room, we could stay at his home for twenty dollars in the hard currency of our choice.

Spending the night in his small, meticulously clean house was disquieting; we sensed the family's quiet heroism as they slept in a small room behind the porch. It was the only way to make a little real money, he explained. It was the only way to be able to provide a brighter future for his family.

The farther into this country we drove, the farther behind the Iron Curtain we traveled, the more I felt dislocated and lost. This was thousands of miles from my culture and thousands of miles from home.

The next morning we arrived in Medias, a small town just north of the Transylvanian Alps. Uncle John and family were waiting. Uncle John, my grandfather's brother, was out to meet us in his wedding coat. It was made of fine lambskin, the leather side out, and embroidered with thousands of stitches of roses and flowers and vines. He smiled broadly, tears streaming down his cheeks.

Someone from the new world had made the long pilgrimage from the West to see him and his family.

He stood on the front step of the small home nestled in the middle of several homes along a muddy street. In raised white stucco above his head was the date 1837. Two large double doors opened onto a small courtyard, and we drove our small rented car inside the enclosure. The family surrounded us with arms outreached and dozens of welcomes. My parents were fluent in their native Saxon, while I could understand a much smaller portion.

Uncle John showed us his three-room house with great pride. He pointed to the two bare electrical lightbulbs glowing dimly in the darkened rooms. The village had gotten electricity in 1969, a few years before our visit.

There were smells, much unlike any I had ever smelled before, swirling in a scented hurricane around us. My uncle pointed to a small clay oven in one corner of the yard, being tended by his daughter. The oven, its fire fed by old corncobs and scrap wood, was heating the flatbreads for our dinner.

Over a small spit next to the oven was the roasting carcass of a young goat they had slaughtered in preparation of our arrival. Chickens pecked nearby, and the stalls at the back of the house separated the house from a large garden behind it.

It was hours before dinner; perhaps we would like to tour the village.

I shouldn't have laughed, but I did. The village was two rutted and muddy streets, a single well, perhaps two dozen homes, a combination village hall/tavern/government offices building, and an old Lutheran church.

What could there be to tour? What was interesting to look at?

In minutes, we had seen the village. Our last stop was the church.

The Romanian government did as much as they could to discourage religious expression, but they allowed the church to remain standing. Uncle John's son-in-law opened the wooden gate, unlocked the thick, oak front door, and motioned my brother and me in.

I hesitated a moment. It had been many years since I had entered a church, and I did not want to be hypocritical. I felt uncomfortable in light of my relative's obvious joy. I wanted to enjoy its beauty from outside. I would be more comfortable looking at the exterior. I am not one prone to mysticism, but I heard a small voice inside telling me to stay out, that this was not a place I belonged.

My cousin would have none of that, and he roughly grabbed my hand and pulled me into the cool, quiet darkness of the small church. Inside, my eyes struggled to penetrate the gloom. There were a few rough-hewn pews, a small handmade altar, a single, small, stained-glass window. The walls were bare and white. To one side of the room was a small doorway leading to the rickety stairs of the steeple tower.

After a few minutes in the silent darkness, my cousin gestured toward the steps and pantomimed a photo being snapped. Again, he ushered me, allowing no hesitation, to the opening. I ducked my head and carefully made my way up the cobwebby passage. The tower looked over the village and toward the gentle foothills of the Carpathians.

It was quiet and still. A patchwork of red and tan roofs quilted the view, each nestled along a garden and fields. Cows were lowing in the distance. A rooster called from below. The fires of a dozen cooking stoves curled into the breezeless afternoon. It was a panoramic glimpse into the eighteenth century.

My cousin turned to me with obvious pride on his face. He explained in grade-school German—the only kind I could understand—that the government wanted to demolish the church following World War II. But there were enough church members in the village to pay the taxes and upkeep for the church.

"Wieviel?" I asked, "How much?"

He scratched his head and said, "Forty-eight eggs a year."

"Eggs?" I asked, afraid that I had misunderstood.

It was all that they could afford, he explained. They sell the eggs at the local market, and the money goes to the church. It was his family's share to keep the building standing. The government allowed no services, no ministers, no Bible studies, but the building stood as a testament to a faith that had not been extinguished by nearly thirty years of repression.

I felt uncomfortable with this faith and uncomfortable in this setting and wanted to be home again.

That evening we enjoyed the roasted goat and bottles of homemade wine. What little they had, they shared with joy. They shared with laughter.

A silence settled, and in the distance we heard the sound of a cowbell, then two, and then others, in a low and rhythmic cadence. Uncle John jumped up and hurried outside to the courtyard. We followed and watched as he lifted off the heavy wooden bar and swung the door open.

In such a poor village, everyone owned some chickens or perhaps a goat or two. If they were a little more successful, they owned a water buffalo. Uncle John owned two of the black, lumbering livestock. Buffalo were raised for milk and eventually meat.

The animal owners pooled their resources and hired one man to tend this motley herd. He went from house to house each morning, gathering his charges. After a day grazing in nearby fields, he would return each to the proper home in the evening.

The herdsman was at Uncle John's door with his two buffalo. The first of Uncle John's animals turned into the courtyard and stopped abruptly. The buffalo looked up at our bright orange Opel Kaddett parked in the open space. The animal looked over at Uncle John, then back to the car, then back over his shoulder to the familiar herdsman.

Why there must be some mistake, the ox must have thought to himself. *This smells right and the*

*fellow on the steps with the white hair looks right,
but there was never a big orange thing here before.
This must be the wrong place.* And with that he
backed out, and his friend behind him backed out
as well.

Uncle John jumped out into the street, grabbed the
ox by the horn, and dragged him in, turning his head
slightly so he wouldn't see all of the car at once. The
herdsman grabbed the second buffalo by the horn,
and likewise turned his head to prevent a full viewing of the car. Within a minute, both animals were in
their stalls for the evening.

I remember that their large brown eyes remained
open wide with disbelief. Their world had suddenly
changed, and they felt alien in this new environment.

I knew how they felt.

I had gone into churches in the past, before I
became a believer, always trying to enter with good
intentions. But each time, there was something that
distracted me. There was always something that happened to make it a one-time visit. I wasn't dressed
appropriately—made very plain by other church
members. The order of service was complicated and
I felt out of place, not knowing what to say or when.
The message was too pointed or not pointed enough.
No one greeted me, or perhaps they greeted me too
warmly. And always there was something inside of
me, uncomfortably tweaking at my conscience.

Each one of us who travel past a church, turning a
wistful eye toward the door, has a hundred reasons
why we should not be inside. Each of us has a long
list of distractions that keep us from crossing the

threshold. My Uncle John knew what to do when his animals were distracted by a bright orange Opel. He turned them away from the distraction and turned their eyes so they only saw the safety of their home.

I am glad that my cousin pulled me inside that humble and worn, old Lutheran church. That experience alone didn't bring me back to God, but it was an essential piece of the mosaic. I wish I had avoided all those sidelong glances that kept me from crossing the threshold. I would have seen the Cross. If I had seen the Cross, I would have felt at home.

Sixteen

The Scar

The way of peace they do not know; there is no justice in their paths. They have turned them into crooked roads; no one who walks in them will know peace. So justice is far from us, and righteousness does not reach us. We look for light, but all is darkness; for brightness, but we walk in deep shadows. Like the blind we grope along the wall, feeling our way like men without eyes. At midday we stumble as if it were twilight; among the strong, we are like the dead. (Isaiah 59:8-10)

Every scar tells a story.

I noticed this one small scar in a fresh way more than a year ago. Early one morning, I was dressing for work. My tie was knotted and in place, except for the two unbuttoned collar buttons. The left one I buttoned with ease. The right one just wouldn't button. I struggled and pushed and tried to maneuver the small white button, but it would not do what a button should—button. I stood in front of the mirror, trying to convince myself that the laundry had done something to shrink just this one buttonhole and make it unfastenable. I was upset. Button-down shirts are supposed to be buttoned down.

I stopped trying, frustrated. I looked down at my left hand and suddenly figured out why this button refused to work. It was my past coming back to haunt me—my present being colored by echoes of my past.

The year was 1974. I was twenty-four years old, had my own apartment, my own car, my own stereo, my own collection of records, my own collection of bills.

I was on my own, armed with a liberal arts degree in English. I was in no hurry to actually use that knowledge and begin a career. What I wanted to do was have fun—to truly experience all that life had to offer. I wanted to be submerged, to be encompassed, to be overwhelmed by life.

This was a time of delirious and delicious freedoms. I was on the cusp of the Woodstock generation and was not bound by my parents' old-fashioned rules and obligations to job, family, God, and country.

I wanted to live for today and do it at full throttle. At twenty-four, life was immense, without boundaries. Tomorrow was but a dream, a poor reason to postpone the pleasures of today.

I was working at an electronics factory on the west side of Minneapolis. I spent hours soldering tiny little wires into tiny little plugs, then building elaborate wire harnesses for complex machinery whose purpose, to me, was an indecipherable mystery. But I enjoyed the work. It was easy, and it required no commitment. I worked a four-day week, ten hours a day. This meant that every week I enjoyed a three-day weekend. The pay was more than adequate to keep me supplied with diversions.

It was December, and winter had come to the Midwest early that year. Calling it cold would be a classic example of an understatement. Imagine how difficult a task it was to get out of a warm bed when the morning weatherman, in a cheerful voice, announced gaily, "It's going to warm up to ten below today."

Winter also meant Christmas. I loved the tinsel and the glitter and the frenzied last-minute panic of buying and wrapping. I loved the giving and the getting—especially the getting. At Thanksgiving, I audited my finances and time. I would spend a week's vacation driving home to Pennsylvania to be with my family. Driving home required gas and food, and there was the rent and the electricity and the gas. What about my "incidentals," my "personal pleasures"? It was the "incidentals" that crimped my plans for other people's presents. If my numbers held up, there would be few presents. And I was not about to limit my pursuit of happiness for a few mere gifts.

I was a creative guy. I should be able to think of something despite my cash-poor position. While pondering, I noticed my neighbor in front of his duplex across the street. A snarling chain saw in hand, he was carving up a dead tree in his parkway. A little lightbulb went off over my head. I threw on a coat, and within minutes I was walking home with a three-foot section of a pine tree—about the diameter of my thigh. I borrowed a handsaw, and within an hour I managed to saw five discs of dry pine, each the size of a small plate and a few inches thick.

I was going to make Christmas gifts this year. I would save money—money that could be spent on me.

I owned a few wood chisels, simple, not sophisticated. I began to chisel and eventually carved out a four-by-six-inch section from the interior of each wooden disc to the depth of a quarter inch or so. It was tricky work, and the chips came slowly.

In just a few afternoons, I had five rustic wood frames. I planned on inserting a photo I had taken of my parents as they rested on a bridge in Würzburg, Germany. It would be a great gift, a future heirloom.

I slipped one of the photos in and gazed at my masterpiece. I began to get depressed. It looked like a bare chunk of tree with a photo pasted on it. Not the impressive heirloom I had first imagined. Disappointed and perplexed, I also realized there was little time to come up with an alternative plan. What if I were to add a bit of decorative carving along the flat surface of the wood? Each frame had several inches of bare wood to work with. Some fancy scroll carving would be easy.

I visited the local hardware store, with its gleaming selection of hammers and pliers and drills and carving implements. There were two carving tools that might work, each with a gray steel blade fashioned in the shape of a V, perhaps three-eighths of an inch wide. One blade was priced at a few dollars, the other one would use up more than an entire twenty-dollar bill, tax included.

"What's the difference between the two?" I asked, anticipating the answer.

"The cheap one is just that: *cheap*," the salesman said. "It won't last long and it's a lot more awkward to use." He paused a moment as he lifted the more costly tool from its case. "Now this one will last for a lifetime." The buttery brown polished wood handle gleamed in the light. "Notice the balance and how well the blade and handle are joined. This blade will keep a sharp edge. It's a lot easier to use and gives better results."

But it was twenty bucks more expensive. The weekend was almost here and I wanted to go out and have a little fun.

"This cheap one will work for a while, won't it?" I asked plaintively as I held the less expensive of the two. "I only have a few little pieces to carve."

The salesman looked blankly at me and slowly nodded. "Yes, it will work for a while," he said. He knew I was not interested in a lifetime investment.

The tool worked fine. And the extra twenty felt good in my wallet. I easily carved the first two frames, chipping and gouging out delicate trails in the wood, in spiral patterns and fleurs-de-lis. After sanding and polishing, the frames were indeed quite striking. Perhaps not heirloom quality, but they looked good.

After a few hours carving, however, I had to admit that the blade wasn't holding a sharp edge. If you oversharpen a cheap blade, it blunts very quickly. It gets more difficult to use. A really good tool holds an edge and stays balanced longer.

Who knew balance? Who knew good tools? So it wasn't balanced, but I was half done. For the price I paid, I could throw it away when I finished and not feel the least bit guilty.

A pile of wood chips grew at my feet, in delicate curls and tight compressed spirals. The trapped resins in the wood filled the room with the faint blush of a winter forest.

I was happy. I was creating something from nothing. The family would be impressed. I was completing the third frame, trying to add a bit more flair to each subsequent piece. The blade stuck in this one for a moment, catching on a small knot. I carefully pried out the wood chip, and slipped the blade back into the groove and pushed again, my left hand bracing the frame against the flat surface of my worktable.

I was soon to learn the absolute importance of balance, the importance of a clean edge. The blade slipped slightly against a harder knot and skittered up out of the narrow groove. I tried to stop my hand's momentum, but in the twinkling of a blade, in the flash of a wood chip falling to the floor, the blade entered the flesh of my index finger at the base and quickly cut through muscles and veins clear to the bone. First, I heard it hit solid matter with a curious chink. A mere instant later there was a more curious metallic snapping as the blade broke off at the handle.

I sat there with my head cocked to one side, much as a dog does when he hears a high-pitched noise for the first time. There was a small metal V protruding from my left hand. *Well,* I calmly thought, *I think I should do something about this.* I should do something before I start hopping up and down and screaming in pain—pain I was certain was only a few seconds away.

I was right. Pain soon reverberated through my hand and my arm up to the shoulder. I grabbed a towel from the bathroom, wrapped it carefully around my hand, blade and all, and ran downstairs to my car. It had a manual transmission, so I drove to the emergency room shifting with my right hand, often steering with my knees.

My entire body was throbbing when I arrived, like a bass drum booming away in sync with my pulse. I could feel the blood seeping through the folds of the towel.

It was Sunday afternoon, a little too early for the emergency room to be swamped with the reckless, the aggressive, and the unlucky. The doctor took a look at my hand, calmly reached for a set of clamps and, in one graceful move, before I could scream, pulled the blade out. It hit the metal tray with an empty metal clang.

"Very nice job," he said with a smile. "Good, clean cut. It will make a nice, even scar, no ragged edges."

After a shot of Novocain, he cleaned the wound, then stitched up the flaps of my skin with the precision of a tailor. He assured me there should be no permanent damage. "It'll hurt for a few days and will probably be numb for a while, but I don't think any major nerves were cut."

Good news, I suppose.

"Don't do any more carving," he suggested.

I promised I wouldn't. Armed with a prescription for painkillers, I drove back home. I stared in amazement at the bloodstains on the wood frame, trailing across the pile of wood chips, and leading into the bathroom.

The doctor was right. The finger was numb for a few days, but the feeling began to return. I was able to do most everything I had done before. I didn't notice any problems. My only souvenir of that day is a very neat L-shaped scar at the first joint of my first finger on my left hand. I seldom thought about it.

But now, nineteen years later, I am feeling the effects of that incident. There is a distinct difference between the two fingers. The finger on my right hand can feel everything from the slightest pressure of a whispered breath to the fractional differences between water that is hot, warm, and just right. It can feel the delicate spines on a bird's feather and the light whisper of the wind as I walk.

The left hand, the left index finger, is different. I feel only the bluntest of pressure, the grossest of changes. I can tell rough from smooth, but merely in a general way. I can tell hot and cold only in extremes.

Maybe the difference between my two fingers was there all the time. Maybe it has gotten more noticeable as I get older. Maybe it was just a tight collar button after all. But perhaps the scar tissue deep in that wound has slowly, a few synapses at a time, choked the feelings from my nerves.

The way we damage our bodies through carelessness makes me think of the way we do the same by another kind of carelessness. Reckless living can bring more serious damage to our souls. At first, there is no pain. We don't feel the cut of the knife, the incisions into the soul. But we age, and scar tissue forms over the wound. Every day there is less and less feeling. The nerve endings are blunted and dulled.

My left finger feels little pain now, but it also has very little sense of touch. A heart left to sin, as mine was, feels very little pleasure or pain. In fact, it feels so very little.

A heart scarred by sin is like ears deafened by too many loud noises. It makes it harder to hear the careful whisper of a meadow on a winter evening, harder to hear the gentle tumbling of snowflakes rubbing together as they fall. It is harder to hear the cry of a newborn baby as he lies in a manger full of straw.

Nineteen years ago I took the road easier traveled. In more ways than just in my woodworking, I picked up tools that were cheap and temporary. I thought little of eternal things. The nerves to my heart were being scarred as well. I had sought out only pleasure for my life.

Though there is now no remedy for my numb finger, there is hope for the scarring that took place in my soul as a result of a lot of carelessness in the past. The remedy comes in the form of the healing power of Christ.

Sometimes God allows our souls to heal with no scarring or nerve damage. But I think sometimes he leaves the scars just to remind us to be careful with the way we live. I know I'll never feel the same way about taking the cheap and easy route. I thank God for forgiveness and restoration. And sometimes I even thank him for the scars.

Seventeen

The Prisoner

For God so loved the world that he gave his one and only Son, that whoever believes in him shall not perish but have eternal life. (John 3:16)

It was the time of hippies and yippies and flower power, a time of teach-ins and sit-ins and demonstrations. Even in blue-collar Pittsburgh, students took to the streets and spoke of revolution and reinventing America. The year was 1971. I was twenty-one years old and enrolled at the University of Pittsburgh.

What a grand time to be a student! We experimented with new forms of cultures. We protested, we marched, we had all the answers. We were in search of our rights and freedoms—freedom to do what we wanted, when we wanted. As long as no one was hurt, why couldn't we run as free as we liked?

The main campus of the university is located in Oakland, just east of downtown Pittsburgh. Between downtown and the school lie the slums of the Hill district. My first apartment was on the border between Oakland and the Hill. I lived, with two other friends, above the Hill Avenue Orthopedic Supply Store. One door down was the Western Pennsylvania School of Mortuary Science. As you might guess, the rent was cheap and the landlord was happily absent.

I majored in English, minored in theater arts. I spent very little time in class, other than theater courses. I never truly considered pursuing a career in acting. I didn't "have to act." However, it was soon very apparent that theater classes were relatively easy, most of the theater people interesting, and their postproduction parties were legendary. What better place to spend your time? The theater can be all-consuming. It was a place to be consumed. It was a home and a family. It was an open, accepting world. We were free from judgments and the hypocrisy of the outside world. We had our art and its truth. And we had the reward and thrill of the applause from an appreciative audience.

I tried out for a few plays, got a couple of small parts. I was a "willing" actor, at best. I was more suited for other theatrical diversions. Over the next several semesters, I built sets, designed lighting, designed and sewed costumes, directed.

I met Dave through the theater. He was short, dark, bearded, moody. He had the desire and talent to become someone else.

The spiritual and geographic center of the University of Pittsburgh is a massive, thirty-story, granite gray medieval cathedral. That's what it's called: the Cathedral of Learning. Intricately carved with spires and gargoyles, it evokes a sense of gloomy history. Hulking over the campus, it held classrooms as well as faculty offices.

Inside the building, on the street level, was a three-story interior. The inside matched the moodiness of the outside. It was a medieval cathedral with a view of the steel mills along the Monongahela River. Stone arches and buttresses and granite columns segmented the dark and musty area into echoes and reverberations. It was full of corners within corners. Dave and I would sprawl on hard, pewlike benches and talk. We would light cigarettes and watch the smoke curl and disappear into the pools of darkness.

Late at night, after rehearsal, we would sit. Footsteps would echo across the dark; sharp voices would carry and fade as doors opened and shut.

Close your eyes slightly and you could imagine being back in time, in an age less enlightened.

As a favor to a friend, I took on the position of assistant director for a student-written play called *The Prisoner*. It was on a bill of three one-act plays. As with most of our student productions, this was staged at the Studio Theater. The Studio was a small teaching theater tucked in a corner of the deepest basement of the Cathedral of Learning. The students ran it as their own and often presented plays from the student body.

The Prisoner told the true story of a man who had been imprisoned alone in a single small cell for decades in a foreign land. The setting was eastern Europe at the turn of the century. The prisoner did not speak the local language and spent most of his adult life having no real contact with the outside world. Year after year, he struggled to be understood, never being able to tell anyone of his feelings, his dreams, his despair, his pain. His story was locked inside of him.

Dave was the prisoner. The role required him to crouch in a small, dark cell, with only a part of his face and his outstretched hands visible. The prisoner tried to communicate with his captors and guards, but they had no interest with him. That is until his last guard. He took an interest and tried to understand his prisoner's odd language, his mimed hand signals, his hesitant gestures to the outside world.

There were only two actors in this one-act play. The three of us rehearsed and rehearsed this little play, memorizing the movements and lines. The actors tried to become their parts. We did this for weeks and weeks, carefully crafting our elegant facade, this illusion of reality.

Dave didn't struggle with his part. "This guy is me," he would say and laugh. "I know who he is."

During the time I knew Dave, we became friends. And I began to hear his pain. He talked about his spiritual alienation. I pointed to Zen and the Eastern philosophies of Alan Watts. He cried when he and his fiancée broke up after a five-year relationship. I pointed him to the music of Bob Dylan and Jim Morrison. His parents threatened to disown him because of his involvement in the theater. I quoted Timothy Leary. Dave and I huddled together and shared our generation's methods of mind expansion. We were free from society's bonds and chains.

I helped him to see the reality of the world, the reality of his existence, the truth of art, and the absolute freedom of the individual. Our generation was exploding the myths of our parents, and we were riding this new wave of freedom. We were the sum of creation, the crown of creation. In us rested perfection. All we had to do was open up to it.

The Prisoner ran for three weekends and received rave reviews from audiences and critics. It was the final play of the night, and its dramatic climax was the stuff of great theater. The prisoner and his last guard had become friends and they had learned to communicate their hopes and dreams to each other. The guard began to understand the prisoner's gestures and odd tongue. The guard began to feel some of the prisoner's pain and despair and tried to offer a small ray of hope through his conversation. Suddenly a change in the government took place. The new ruler decreed that all political prisoners were to be eliminated. Dave pantomimed being dragged from his cell, his hands clutching at the bars. Orders and

commands bellowed from loudspeakers behind the
stage. Tom, who played the old guard, watched with
hollow eyes as his new friend was dragged away,
boots echoing in the hall behind the stage.

The stage grew dark and still. From the recesses
behind the cell, a beating drum called out a cadence.
Then a loud voice called out: "Ready, Aim, Fire."

And I, standing in the darkness, would point a
starter pistol, loaded with blanks, in the air and fire.
The gunshot sounded like a cannon in such a small
theater. The audience would leap in surprise and
shock. A dim spotlight illuminated the guard's face
as tears would come to his eyes. And the light would
fade to black. It was the epiphanic moment of the
production. Just before the light was gone, the old
guard would say, in a halting voice, "It wasn't my
fault. I could not stop them. Good-bye, friend. I will
miss you."

The last night of the play's run both actors had
their roles edged with a truth that was rare in a
student production. The audience was on the edge
of their seats.

The prisoner was dragged out of the cell, his hands
pleading with his friend to help him, to prevent this
crime from happening.

The voices called, and the drums rolled. I raised
the gun with one hand, and I still do not know how I
managed to do what I did next. As I pulled the trigger, the gun slipped in my grasp slightly, and I rushed
my other hand to steady it—and the gun's hammer
snapped shut on the fleshy part between my thumb
and forefinger.

In that mere second before I pulled the trigger again and freed my hand, I experienced the most shocking and intense pain I had ever felt, as the hammer literally crushed this sensitive area. Blood filled my hand. There was nothing I could do. I couldn't scream in front of a full theater. Stars and white lights seemed to fill my head, and my breath grew short. The taped message was given to fire, and I pulled the trigger just in time to scare the audience once again.

Have you ever shaken a soda bottle, shaken it so hard, that the carbonated gases literally blew the cap off? That was how my head felt. It was about to explode from the unreleased pain. In that split second I realized there was absolutely nowhere to take the pain—there was no way of making the pain smaller—there was no way of lessening the immediacy of the pain that filled my being.

The lights came up, the actors stepped out from behind the curtain, the audience began to applaud, and I doubled over and tried to surround my hand with my body while silently screaming over and over.

A handful of aspirin, a bag of ice, and I began to recover.

The next morning we took the set down. Dave helped, but stared off into space as we worked. He looked alone and lost.

"Do you want to talk? Is something bothering you?" I asked. "Maybe we can sit down after we're done today." In an hour or so, the set was dismantled, and I had a class, and he had a class and we would catch up later. Besides, I had given him all my best advice. He knew what to do with his troubles.

Two days later, he went into his bathroom, locked the door . . . and slit his throat with a razor.

It has been more than twenty years since this happened, and as I tell this story, my chest tightens, my heart races, and the words get caught in my throat. I have looked back at this event so very often, trying to make sense of it. I now realize that Dave's life was full of the same kind of pain that I experienced in that instant as the hammer tore into my hand. And his pain—like mine—had no real outlet. It stayed inside, bottled up. My pain was just physical. But his pain was in his heart.

Why did my friend do it? Why did he take the ultimate escape? Were things that bad? Why didn't I see it coming?

I don't really know. Some "why" questions are impossible for us to answer. Why did he do it? Why did he let the pain overwhelm him? Why did he choose such an angry escape?

Twenty years ago I thought I had the answers. But I had no answer for Dave—or for anyone, for that matter.

If Dave were still here, I would point to the Cross. I would point to the absolute certainty of Christ and to the truth that he purchased us with his sacrifice. I could assure him that God is in control. We may not understand the "why" of events, but God does. He offers relief to that pain.

The suffering of one college student twenty years ago is not inconsequential. It meant something to me. It changed me. It means something to God. If this story reaches one person who needs to hear about God's gift, then perhaps, just perhaps, that is the "why" of all this.

Too often we think that a friend who is sad or lonely can "snap out of it" by themselves. "If they are Christian, then God will help them out of their depression." It is not that easy. And we must remember that God uses us to accomplish things. And think of the pain, how much worse it is, for those people who do not have Jesus to turn to.

This is more than just a sad story. I miss Dave, and I am sad that I missed the opportunity to help alleviate his pain. I have come to realize that I was a prisoner of sin, just like the prisoner behind bars that Dave played. If someone back then had shared the right words, Dave might still be with us. One of the most important parts of being a Christian is that: sharing the Good News with a dark and desperate world filled with prisoners.

Eighteen

Lost

Suppose one of you has a hundred sheep and loses one of them. Does he not leave the ninety-nine in the open country and go after the lost sheep until he finds it? And when he finds it, he joyfully puts it on his shoulders and goes home. Then he calls his friends and neighbors together and says, "Rejoice with me; I have found my lost sheep." I tell you that in the same way there will be more rejoicing in heaven over one sinner who repents than over ninety-nine righteous persons who do not need to repent. (Luke 15:4-7)

Lost!

Being lost can either be an exciting adventure with new experiences or a terror-filled episode, full of pain, fear, and stress. The ultimate outcome often depends on who you are.

Being lost produces an array of gender-related subtleties. According to my extensive research, both the male and female of the species are similar in their ability to lose their way. It's just that the male will never admit to that fact. Only under the most desperate situations will he stop and ask where he is and where it is he is supposed to be. If the man does ask for directions, he will forget all but the first two turns by the time he rolls up the car window.

It may be genetic, but it is also often a learned behavior. I remember sitting in the backseat of the family car while my father drove for what seemed like days to get across town to visit relatives. Vacation trips seemed even longer. When my mother would ask if my father knew where he was, my father would inevitably reply, "Of course I know where I am. I'm right here in this car!"

And to my father's credit, we almost always got to where we needed to go. And he was never nervous about an extra mile or two of traveling time in order to accomplish the goal. He loved to explore, and a wrong turn merely added a new discovery to life, a new road to explore.

But there was one time when being lost was not just an adventure but a much larger, much darker experience.

The year was 1956.

I was six years old. It was summer, and summer meant one thing.

Lake Erie.

Our family owned a small lakeside cottage on the southern shore of the lake and a few miles west of the city of Erie.

It was indeed a summer cottage—a very small cottage, with two bedrooms, a sleeping porch, a small bath, an even smaller kitchen, and a great room with a fireplace.

The cottage was in a curious spot on the lake. No roads led to it. The only way to reach it was to park the car on an open, graveled area along a narrow and seldom-used paved road, and then descend, to what felt to a six-year-old like a mile-long journey into the dark, through a dense and foreboding forest, and finally step out on the lakeshore and the cabin and the sunlight. The footpath followed a small stream and cut through a dense pine and oak grove, the roots of the trees coming to the surface along the path, ready to reach out and trip unwary children. There was also no direct access to the four or five dozen other cottages on that stretch of beach. This may be an unusual situation today, but back in the fifties, it was not.

My mother and my brothers and sister and I would stay at the cottage the entire summer, while my father would commute back and forth on the weekends.

One of the problems with this spot was that the entire summer's worth of supplies—bedding, clothes, kitchen supplies, food, toys, and everything else we needed for the three months—had to be hand-carried down that small narrow path.

"How many more trips do we need to make?" was the common refrain, sometimes said in frustration, but more often said as the family's summer joke. Cots, pots and pans, food bags, duffel bags, rubber rafts, and radios were gathered from the back of the station wagon or rooftop and hauled down the path, often in near darkness, to be dumped in the great room of the musty cabin.

We left very few items in the cottage over the winter. Its isolation and weak security system were an invitation to the occasional weekend burglar.

Eventually we would make the three or four or twenty trips up and back, up and back.

This extended portage, this caravaning of supplies, was a small price to pay for a summer of magic. Lake Erie and this humble, tiny cottage were truly magical places to a six-year-old. The house was shaded by a dozen oak trees. A white sand beach curved along the shore for as far as the eye could see. The lake waves lapped against the shore only a couple of dozen yards in front. An old tree, most of its limbs cut away, the bark stripped by the winter storms, lay between the house and the shore, parallel to the water. It became a raft and a pirate ship and a rocket ship and a backstop and a bench for an evening bonfire.

The woods behind the cabin were full of clay caves and streams and delicate hidden spots that overlooked the glassy lake, which stretched all the way to Canada. It was a time of total freedom to explore, to swim, to fish.

Paradise for a six-year-old.

One other element stood above every other attraction and made this time, this place, this environment totally and completely wonderful.

Waldameer Park.

Waldameer, in German, means "Woods by the Sea." I am sure that Waldameer Park began, at the turn of the century perhaps, as a sylvan glade of woods, parceled out and preserved as a picnic spot, overlooking the shores of the lake. Groups would have come, with picnic hampers and starched collars, to spend a pleasant Sunday afternoon, perhaps listening to a polka band.

A band shell strung with colorful lights provided a place for waltzing in the smooth dusk of a warm evening by the lake. Perhaps a picnic shelter was added next, and maybe a small restaurant or beer hall. And then for the kids, a merry-go-round or a pony ride.

By the time our family arrived, midcentury, Waldameer was a jewel box of an amusement park, a small gem on the shores of the lake.

And we could walk to it. Imagine that—an amusement park within walking distance.

Out of our cabin, turn right, east toward town, and walk along the beach, staring at other cabins we passed. People named their cabins back then to reflect the individuality of the owners. On our way to the park, we passed "The House That Jack Built," which was built with two cement piers anchoring the front porch and the rear of the house nestled into the bluff behind. It was washed away during the winter storms of 1957, and all that remained were the two silent concrete piers, standing like ghosts at the water's edge. Up the bluff was an unnamed bunkerlike building with cement sidewalks that were excellent for catching toads during an evening rain. On the way to the park, one would pass "The Full House," "The Waves," "Open to the Air," "The Ark," "It's About Time," and "Queens Four," regal names in front of two- and three-room summer cottages. It was an optimistic and happy stretch of beachfront in 1956.

About a mile up the beach—perhaps a mile and a half—you came to a small cold-water stream that for years had a bent-over birch tree that spanned from shore to shore. The adventurous would climb across, delicately balancing on slick bark, often splashing in halfway across. Adults with any sense would simply take off shoes and socks, roll up pant legs, and wade across the calf-high waters.

Another few hundred feet and there was a path of sorts, a primitive road to a primitive, but free, boat launch. That is where you turned inland and walked a quarter mile or so to reach the park. By this time you could hear the faint music, the rumble of the rides, the screams of the riders—tiny echoes of joy in the breeze.

It was a quarter mile of increasing, palatable, almost quivering anticipation for a six-year-old.

I have hesitated to ever return to Waldameer Park, although I know it still exists, for fear of what I might find. But in 1956, to this six-year-old, it was the perfect blending, the perfect synthesis, of rides, games, food, and thrills. It provided an elegant and exotic atmosphere, mixing the forbidden with the permitted, the known with the unknown.

It has been thirty-six years since I walked into that park, yet I can hear it and taste it as if it were yesterday. Parts of it are still visible in my memory. There was the Old Mill ride, an outdoor canal waterway navigated by gaily painted and intricately carved wooden boats, each carrying eight passengers. The elegant vessels gently floated through a serene garden of roses and pines. At the very end, the boat would be grabbed by a rubber belt and lifted higher and higher into the air and then plummeted down at breathtaking speed to a foaming pool.

In reality, it most likely was no higher than a ten- or fifteen-foot descent, and unlike the water rides at today's amusement parks, no one ever got wet. But for its time, it was state-of-the-art excitement. I was in line for my third or fourth ride when a little blonde girl tried to enter the line behind me with her mother in tow. "Please, Mom, please," the girl begged. Her mother eyed the boats as they plunged into the pool at the end of the ride, looked at her daughter's upturned and pleading face, and slowly shook her head. "No, dear," she explained. "This ride is too wild and woolly for me." And they turned away to seek gentler pursuits, the child's head turned, over her shoulder, toward the ride with a desperate longing in her eyes.

A roller coaster rumbled over a rickety bridge— right over the road into the park. The park also had a merry-go-round, a small penny arcade, a Tilt-A-Whirl, and several other rides. There were concessions and cotton-candy booths.

But the memory of one time during the summer of 1956 was not so pleasant and carefree. It was the time when I understood what it was to be lost.

It was July, sometime around the Fourth. Our family was at the cottage, and my father's sister Sophia, her husband, Bill, and their three children were there. Perhaps because the memory of this is a bit like quicksilver, my mother's divorced brother was there, too, with his daughter.

A quick head count yields fifteen family members, in a house designed to hold no more than five or six.

It was great delirious fun to be in the hurricane of relatives, laughing, cooking, eating, swimming, listening to the old family stories in the evening, stories about Pap, my grandfather.

On this day, midafternoon, as I remember, most likely to break free of the confines of the small cottage, it was decided that the whole clan would march down the beach, head east, and spend a pleasant afternoon at the park.

I am sure all the children danced around the adults as we set off in our caravan, jumping and yelling like excited puppies at the prospect of a walk.

Later that summer afternoon, as the sun started to settle toward the west, my adult relatives gathered their tired, sticky children and began the slower, quieter walk west back to the cottage, back to dinner, back to an evening watching the lake waters curl toward shore and then ebb back again.

Five adults and ten children began the walk, and according to the laws of fluid hydraulics, the line of walkers compacted, stretched out, compacted again, as each individual would try to match the gait of the person in front. Or clumps of twos and threes would break off, their voices hushed to a whisper as they exchanged opinions on child rearing. And small clusters of children would dart off to the water's edge to peer at a dead fish, or over to the high-water mark on the shore to look for interesting driftwood. I often marched at the head of the pack, for even at that age I was not very good at following others in a crowd.

Accountability was lax. Everyone enjoyed the cool breezes as the sun dipped closer to the watery horizon.

As dusk settled, the cottage snuggled into view, and dinner plans were discussed with increasing excitement. Kids peeled off this way to the water and that way to the woods, and parents and aunts and uncles settled down on the screened porch to rest older feet and bones.

Everyone was safe.

That is, all except one. All except the six-year-old who fancied himself a leader. The six-year-old who thought himself a pirate, a go-it-alone swashbuckler, who happened to be just a bit too far ahead of the rest.

I must have been staring out to sea as the cottage came into view. I must have been looking for fireflies as I carefully walked past the cottage, I must have been searching for the silhouettes of lake freighters against the setting sun as I resolutely marched forward. I must have been dreaming about being free to roam the Great Lakes on a raft I was building in the woods behind the cottage. I must have been . . .

Wait a minute!

I stopped and stared ahead. That stretch of beach did not look right. There were far fewer cottages here, and, out of the corner of my eyes, without wanting to turn around, I could see the looming presence of a massive seawall, built of rusting steel girders and cement to protect the shoreline. It was towering over me. There was no seawall where we lived.

I wheeled about, and in a terrifying flash of awareness, I saw the beach behind me to the east, empty and dark for as far as I could see. The sand trailed off into the horizon and the blackness of the coming night. There were no parents, no aunts, no uncles, no cousins.

Just the sound of the water pushing toward the shore.

I was alone. And I was very, very lost.

Yes, I know now that there was only one way to go to get back home. But that six-year-old was not so sure. Was there a turnoff that I was supposed to take? Did we always turn left or right somewhere and I never paid attention to it? And why would no one have noticed me being gone? Where did I think I was going?

And how would I ever get home again?

I am sure that tears filled my eyes and terror filled my heart. I stood, paralyzed, as the long shadows turned the lake into a dark, ink black, rolling menace, with watery arms reaching out to draw me under. I stood there as the woods to the south turned black and ominous and screeched out my name in a thousand croaking voices.

"You're lost! You're lost," they cried, "and you will never be safe again. You will never see your mother and father again. You will never see your dog again. You are lost forever."

And I was sure that I was. I was sure that I was lost forever.

I stood there, limp, crying . . . sobbing because I did not know where to go to escape this terror. I had absolutely no idea of how to be saved, how to get "unlost."

The strip of sand I was on, between the icy deep waters of the lake to the north and the tangled swamps and thorns of the forest to the south, seemed to shrink, and soon I seemed to be standing—no, balancing—on this thin precipice between the devil and the deep blue sea, and the devil was on both sides of me.

I looked up, and through the salt of my tears, through the blurred terror of my vision, I saw a thin pencil beam of light, sweeping slowly across the sand, sweeping slowly from water's edge to wood's edge. And then there was another light and another—perhaps a kerosene lantern held at arm's length overhead.

And voices, carrying on the evening breeze—my name being called out, over and over.

My memory shuts down at that point. I was rescued, and I am sure there was both rejoicing and reprimanding that evening. But all that mattered to me was that I was safe—scooped up into the arms of someone who loved me enough to search for me and find me.

I had been lost, and those who could have saved me earlier—they turned away, preoccupied and safe. I was lost, forging ahead, oblivious, into the unknown. I did not, nor could not, realize how far from safety I had gone.

For a child, it is a terrible feeling to be lost. The same terror, however, can fill the bravest adult when he finds himself away from anything familiar and with no idea of which direction to turn to get back to safety. The Bible talks of lost sheep and how terrifying it must be for a lost lamb when darkness falls.

The prophet Isaiah described all mankind as lost sheep that had gone astray. Whether we realize it or not, if we are wandering the world without the Good Shepherd as our guide, we are lost—just as lost, as far as the safety of heaven is concerned, as the six-year-old who strayed from safety. Those who know about the place of safety are like my parents and aunts and uncles and brothers and sisters. They could have saved me—if they had been watching as I strayed off, if they had been looking for me, if they had known that I was lost.

To those walking toward danger, toward the dark and the unknown on the shores of life, if you aren't careful, you will become lost as I did that evening. Turn around and look. You who have kept walking on the wrong path, take courage, for you don't have to be lost forever. There is safety in Jesus, and like my aunts and uncles, he is out looking for you, shining his light and calling your name, inviting you to come back home with him.

Others of us need to be more careful to watch for others who are straying away, getting themselves more and more lost. Get your flashlights, put your shoes back on, and get back on the darkening beach to find those who are walking off in the wrong direction into deeper darkness. We must all be about the business of beachcombing for those who are in the dark, alone, frightened, and in tears.

We must.

Epilogue

An epilogue, marking the end of a literary journey, announces to the world that the story is over and the actors gone home.

I will not draw the curtain today. This epilogue will offer no finality by having these stories tied into a tidy little bundle because the story hasn't ended yet. God is still very much at work in my life—in all of our lives. He is still revealing his truth, showing his presence, displaying his love. That truth provides one of the true joys of having a relationship with God—knowing he is there with us during the dark as well as the light.

So very often, as happened in many of these stories, God's handiwork, his involved presence, is not detected until much later. The crises pass, the pain subsides, the grief turns to acceptance, and we pause to catch our emotional breath, tenderly holding these experiences in our hands. Later, as we look at that little chip of our life, we first see a faint sparkle. As our eyes open wider, the spark expands to fill the entire horizon with the glory of God. He was there with us, holding us, loving us, teaching us, caring for us. The reason that we often are blind to God's workings during the epiphanic moments of life lies in our own human frailty.

I hope that these chips of my life, these meager stories have provided a glint of God's perfect workings in a life. The person I am today was shaped by hundreds of incidents like the ones recounted in this book. I hope others will begin to recognize God's handiwork and begin to appreciate the life-changing and life-shaping dimension of the truth of our Creator. Not only does God work in the lives of those who kneel to his glory, God also works in the lives of those who have not yet opened their eyes wide enough. He works in the lives of those who have chosen not to hear, not to see, not to feel his presence.

There is one truth that I would like to leave with you—the fact that God is revealing himself to everyone at every moment. And what would I have you do with this? Be a friend to those who do not know him yet. Share with them the difference God has made in your life. Help them see God's grace, his power, his love.

We must be about the business of sharing the truth of our God. It is not just a calling—it is the highest calling.

Additional titles of inspiration from Tyndale House Publishers

THE BEST STORIES FROM GUIDEPOSTS   0-8423-0340-5

GLIMPSES OF HIS GLORY
John and Elizabeth Sherrill   0-8423-1082-7

MORE STORIES FROM GUIDEPOSTS   0-8423-4560-4

SPLENDOR IN THE ORDINARY
Brian R. Coffey   0-8423-5934-6

WHEN GOD BREAKS THROUGH
John and Elizabeth Sherrill   0-8423-1129-7

Contents

Assault

**Brigadier Anthony Farrar-Hockley
DSO MBE MC**

The Allied victory in 1945, so successful, so complete, tends to diminish our memories of the early years of the Second World War when, far from seeing a prospect of victory, almost every horizon reflected tidings of continued defeat.

In these years of disaster and loss, what sustained us was a sense of outrage, and hence a determination to recover what had been taken from us – not matter how long it took or how much of our lifeblood was involved.

Such an end could only be attained ultimately by offensive action. In the early summer of 1940, Britain was attempting to organise as best it could, its defeated army and its weak air force to resist the next anticipated phase of Nazi aggression: invasion of the United Kingdom. The stocks of arms and equipment and the numbers of trained men in Britain, were inadequate to meet the needs of home defence together with the rising calls for reinforcement of the Middle East – so no one might seriously suppose that the time was ripe for offensive operations against the occupied coast across the Channel, or against the hostile coastline which stretched up through Denmark to the tip of Norway in the Arctic circle.

Nonetheless, some men were thinking of immediate offensive action even while British troops were still crossing over from Dunkirk. Recog-

nising that attack on the grand scale was out of the question, the Prime Minister and others were ready to accept temporarily a lesser form: raiding.

As ever, a new concept, a new organisation tends to be resisted, even at a peak of crisis in a nation's affairs. Thus the idea of a special raiding organisation, of units specially recruited and organised for this work, tended to be opposed, sometimes deliberately obstructed. Fortunately, the influence of the Prime Minister and the enthusiasm of a sufficient number of soldiers, sailors and airmen, brought into being the Commandos.

Brigadier Peter Young is a founder-member of this select body. What he has written is a short history of their activities from inception to the Dieppe Raid of August 1942. Not surprisingly, it reads like an adventure story; for that is what the Commandos engaged in – a series of grim adventures from which a high number did not return. Their adventures not only raised the alarm along the occupied coast line – they raised the morale of the Allied sympathisers everywhere, progressively, as the scope and the range of their operations spread from Europe to the Mediterranean coastlines.

The units wearing the green beret became legendary. Brigadier Young's narrative tells us why.

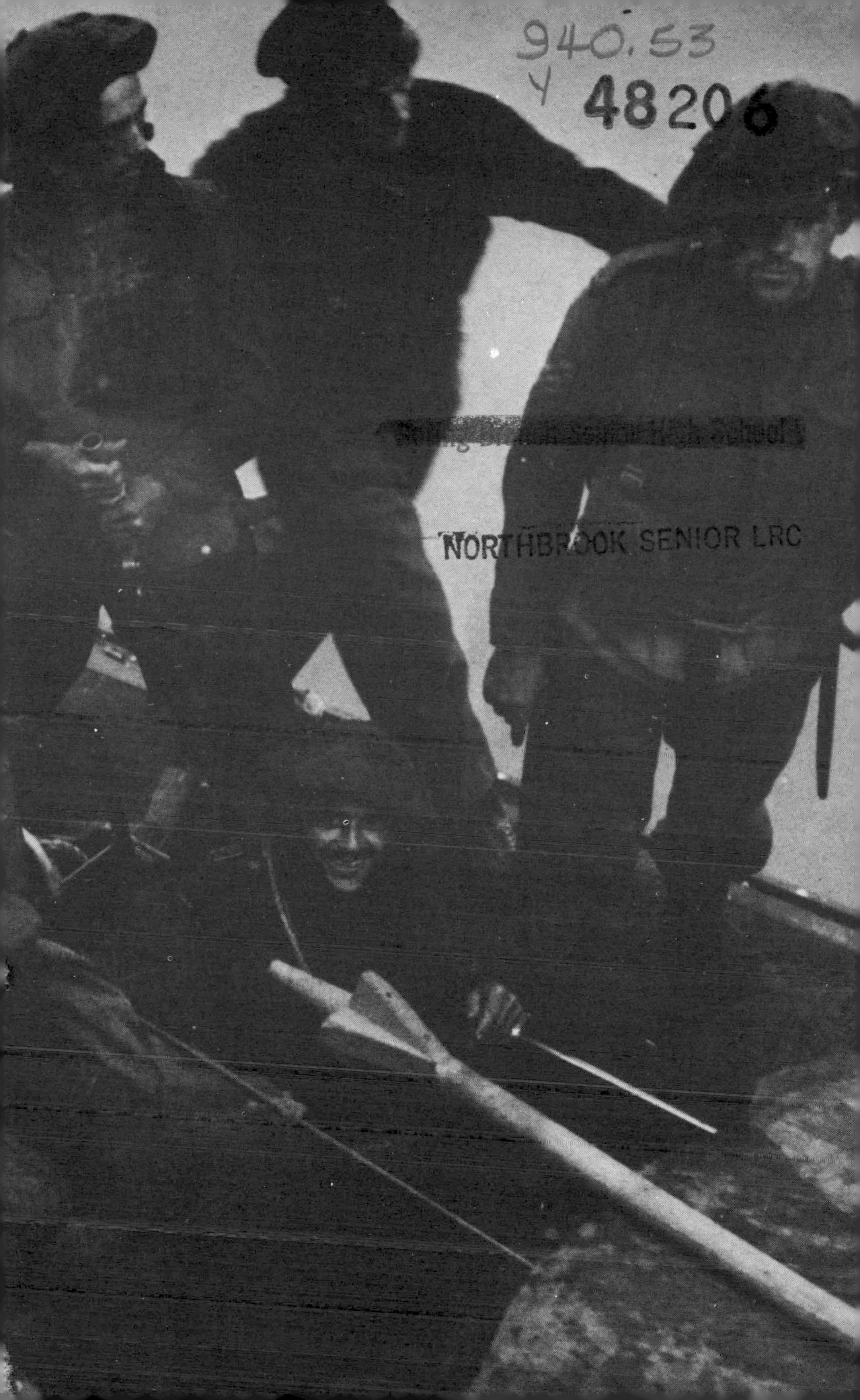

Editor-in-Chief: Barrie Pitt
Art Director: Peter Dunbar

Military Consultant: Sir Basil Liddell Hart
Picture Editor: Robert Hunt

Executive Editor: David Mason
Art Editor: Sarah Kingham
Designer: John Marsh
Cover: Denis Piper
Research Assistant: Yvonne Marsh
Cartographer: Richard Natkiel
Special Drawings: John Batchelor

Ballantine Books Inc.
101 Fifth Avenue, New York, NY 10003
An Intext Publisher

The beginnings

'Of course, it is absolutely terrific. It is the greatest job in the Army that one could possibly get, and it is a job that, if properly carried out, can be of enormous value . . . no red tape, no paper work . . . just pure operations, the success of which depends principally on oneself and the men one has oneself picked to do the job with you . it's revolutionary.'

The man who invented the Commandos was Lieutenant-Colonel Dudley Clarke. In the grim Dunkirk days he was Military Assistant to the Chief of the Imperial General Staff, General Sir John Dill. Pondering the defeat of the Allies in France and Belgium he wrestled with one of the age old problems of warfare: what does a nation do, when, though its army has been beaten in the field, it does not accept the decision? His mind ranged back to the guerrilla warfare against Napoleon's armies in Spain, and to the Arab Revolt in Palestine, where he himself had served in 1936. 'Could desperate men, armed only with the weapons they could carry, disdaining artillery, baggage trains and all the

paraphernalia of supply, carry on guerrilla warfare against an enemy whose forces were stretched out from Narvik to the Pyrenees?' (From *The Green Beret* by H St George Saunders.) This was the problem, and before retiring to bed on 4th June – the last of the nine days of Dunkirk – the colonel sat down in his flat in Stratton Street, Mayfair, and marshalled his ideas 'in note form on a single sheet of writing paper.'

To anyone accustomed to the normal workings of government the next stage of the story is little short of fantastic: 5th June: Clarke tells Dill his idea. 6th June: Dill tells Winston Churchill, the Prime Minister. 8th June: Dill tells Clarke the scheme is approved and that afternoon, Section MO9 of the War Office is brought into being.

Dudley Clarke was ordered to mount a raid across the Channel 'at the earliest possible moment'. The only conditions laid down by the Prime Minister were that no unit should be diverted from its most essential task, the defence of Britain, which might

Lieutenant-Colonel Dudley Clarke

Above: General Sir John Dill and Winston S Churchill at a tank demonstration in May 1941. *Right:* The Commando spirit

very soon have to face invasion, and that the guerrillas would have to be content with the minimum quantity of weapons. Both of these conditions were inevitable in the circumstances of the time, and otherwise Clarke was given a free hand.

The Prime Minister's interest and support was a vital factor in imparting a sense of urgency to those concerned with their formation. His thinking is revealed in a minute of 18th June 1940: 'What are the ideas of the C-in-C Home Forces, about 'Storm Troops' or 'Leopards' drawn from existing units, ready to spring at the throat of any small landings or descents? These officers and men should be armed with the latest equipment, tommy guns, grenades, etc., and should be given great facilities in motor-cycles and armoured cars.'

The next problem was to raise a raiding force. This could either be done by taking existing battalions

from Home Forces or by raising fresh units. The latter solution was adopted, a decision which for various reasons was a wise one. Commanding officers and a number of the company commanders were in their forties, decidedly on the old side for raiding. The ranks of units belonging to Home Forces were full of reservists and young conscripts, some too cautious and others too inexperienced to guarantee results in operations where 'the book' – Field Service Regulations – would provide no guidance, and where the deadly and the impossible would be normal. Moreover, the war establishment (or organization) of a standard infantry battalion, designed to take its place in a prolonged campaign, was not necessarily the most suitable for a light raiding force. Considerations of this sort led to the decision to form a new style unit, the Commando. Its name was taken from mobile Boer units, which for some two years had defied 250,000 British troops during the Boer War (1899-1902). The original organization, a headquarters and ten troops each of three officers and forty-seven other

ranks, owed nothing to the establishment of a battalion. If anything it harked back to the 18th Century rangers and light corps which made their names under men like Rogers, Marion 'the Swamp Fox', Ewald, and Tarleton.

The cadre of Numbers 1 and 2 Commandos came from the ten Independent Companies raised earlier in the year when the Germans invaded Norway. They were composed for the most part of volunteers from the Territorial Army, and were intended to raid the enemy lines of communication. As things turned out they had done no raiding though about half of them had seen action fighting desperate rearguard actions in the snowclad valleys around Bodo and Mo.

The other commandos were formed by calling for volunteers for special service. Commanding officers were selected from among the volunteers. They were then given a free hand to choose their own officers. Thereafter the three officers of each troop drove round the various units allotted to them and recruited their own men.

This rough and ready system worked pretty well. The original commanding officers included Bob Laycock from the Royal Horse Guards; John Durnford-Slater from the Royal Artillery; and Ronnie Tod from the Argyll and Sutherland Highlanders. Before the war ended the first of these was to become a major-general and Chief of Combined Operations, while the last two became brigadiers.

The letter which outlined the conditions of this special service was not particularly revealing. One officer who joined at the outset recalls that: 'Commanding Officers were to ensure that only the best were sent; they must be young, absolutely fit, able to drive motor vehicles, and unable to be seasick. It was a leap in the dark, for absolutely nothing was said as to what they were to do, and in any case most regular officers make a point of never volunteering for anything.' Be that as it may, no less than ten of the original officers of Number 3 Commando were regulars. One of the conditions of service, clearly laid down, was that any man might voluntarily return to his unit, after an operation. Few ever asked to do so.

Indeed to be RTU (returned to unit) was the fate most dreaded by Commando soldiers.

Something like one hundred troops were formed and practically every regiment and corps of the British Army must have been represented. Regulars, reservists and territorials from every part of the country were to be found in their ranks and one can hardly say that any troop was typical. H Troop of Number 3 Commando, in which the present writer served, was selected from men of the 4th Division, which had fought with some tenacity in the Dunkirk campaign. The men, though they included soldiers from the Royal Artillery, the Royal Engineers and the Royal Army Service Corps, were for the most part selected from the county regiments, the backbone of the British Infantry. For the most part they were reservists, but there was a leavening of regulars. The majority had served in India, and were skilled men-at-arms. They had been in action and wanted more. This troop was perhaps exceptional, but all were determined to excel. Before June was out this Commando had assembled at Plymouth, and all over the country the new units were springing to life.

Not the least remarkable of the many strange things about the history of the Commandos is that their first raid took place only nineteen days after their formation. It cannot be claimed that it was an epoch-making event, but at least it was a step on the long road back to Europe, the road to victory.

The planning of military operations is never precisely easy, even without the added complication of a sea crossing. The planning of raids in the summer of 1940 presented well-nigh every obstacle that the most pessimistic planner's nightmares could conjure up. But the men who conceived the Commandos were optimists. In the summer when Winston Churchill was inspiring his countrymen with promises of blood, sweat, toil and tears, pessimism, however well founded, was not in season. It was just as well. To plan a raid one needs a wide choice of suitable targets, and accurate information as to enemy forces and their deployment in the area of the objective. Up to June 1940 all the resources of British Intelligence had been concentrated on the German build-up on the Western Front. Now the coast of Europe from Narvik to Bayonne had suddenly become the enemy line and the slow piecing together of information, from the reports of agents and from air photography, had to begin all over again.

When Dudley Clarke first went to seek the co-operation of the Admiralty he was cordially received by the Assistant Chief of the Naval Staff: 'What! The Army wants to get back to fight again already? That's the best news I've had for days. For that you can have anything you like to ask for from the Navy.' Captain G A Garnons-Williams was given the task of collecting craft and set up his headquarters in the yacht *Melisande* lying in the Hamble. Motor boats and pleasure craft of every description, and widely differing reliability, were assembled from the Norfolk Broads and anywhere else where in peacetime people had enjoyed themselves 'messing about in boats'.

Willing though the Navy was, combined operations demanded landing-craft, and the very few Britain had possessed in 1939 had been lost in Norway. Still, a service that had so recently improvised a flotilla to bring 338,226 British and French troops from Dunkirk was not unduly troubled by the problem of taking a few hundred men in the other direction. If they had to land from unarmoured craft designed for entirely different purposes, the soldiers did not care – if only because they didn't know any better.

The naval side of planning an operation is complicated by problems of navigation, wind and tide. There are often no more than a few days in any month when a particular beach or landing place will be practicable. When so many things can go wrong it is just as well to load the dice as much as possible. This in itself is sufficient justification for seeing to it that the troops employed are all picked volunteers.

The first commando raid was carried out on the night of 23rd/24th June, when landings were made in the Boulogne-Le Touquet area. Major Tod was in command of the force, 120 strong, which bore the title of Number 11 Independent Company. Garnons-Williams had managed to borrow half a dozen RAF rescue craft from the Air Ministry. Though fast, reliable, and seaworthy, their bows were high out of the water and therefore they were not ideal for landing craft.

The expedition, whose armament included half of the forty Tommy guns then in the country, sailed from Dover, Folkestone and Newhaven. In mid-Channel Spitfires swooped down to examine them, but fortunately realizing they they were not German patrol boats, refrained from shooting them up. However, this incident caused some delay.

The air-sea rescue craft lacked sophisticated navigational devices, and Tod was on the point of entering Boulogne harbour when an enemy searchlight suddenly revealed the position. They made off down the coast and landed in some sand dunes, where they had an indecisive brush with a German patrol. The only casualty was Dudley Clarke, who had accompanied the expedition as an observer. A bullet struck him a glancing blow and nearly severed an ear. Thus it chanced that the man who conjured up the idea of the Commandos was the first of them to be wounded.

Another party landed at the Plage de Merlimont, four miles south of Le Touquet, and attacked a large building surrounded by a deep belt of barbed wire. They killed the two sentries and then, unable to make their way through the wire, threw Mills grenades through the windows. Whether the building was a billet, an officers' mess or a headquarters cannot be said, but one may assume that the inmates were not pleased.

At Dover the returning craft were cheered by every ship in the harbour, at Folkestone the arrival of thirty dishevelled soldiers was regarded with the utmost suspicion. In the country in general the bald announcement that, less than a month after Dunkirk, the British had, as it were, stuck a pin into Hitler, was well received.

MO9 lost no time in thinking up another thrust. On the night of the 14th/15th July a raid was mounted against the German garrison of Guern-

13

The first Commando raids, which took place in the summer of 1940. The first was launched soon after the formation of the Commandos and resulted in only a skirmish with the occupation forces, but the second, on Guernsey, was a failure, though lessons were learnt in both raids.

HMS Scimitar

sey. This time the intelligence provided was rather impressive. The Germans had been flown in on 1st July, and were 469 strong under a Doktor Maas – their ration strength had been revealed to one of our agents by the contractor.

The force included Major Tod's 11 Independent Company which was to attack the airport, and H Troop, Number 3 Commando, which was to make a feint attack against a machine-gun position at Telegraph Bay and the barracks on the Jerbourg peninsula.

The force was carried in two rather ancient destroyers, *Scimitar* and *Suladin* (1918 vintage) and the landing craft were seven RAF rescue craft. The planning by the newly organized Directorate of Raiding Operations was impressive. It was arranged that Ansons should fly over the island to drown the noise of the landing-craft as they ran in.

The raid was mounted from the Gymnasium of the Naval College, Dartmouth, and some of the cadets helped to load the Tommy gun magazines. An officer who took part in the raid writes: 'After tea in the college dining room we boarded HMS *Scimitar*. Only five of the rescue craft had turned up. We proceeded to sea, increased speed to eighteen knots, and shaped a course for Guernsey. About midnight the rescue craft, which had been keeping station about one hundred

yards away, came alongside and the soldiers transferred to them as silently as possible. The rescue craft made a terrible noise and the sound of the Ansons flying low over Jerbourg peninsula to drown our noise was most welcome. These craft were very high out of the water; moreover, we were very crowded. The idea of coming under aimed small-arms fire in such a craft was unattractive, but no machine gun opened up.'

In fact the Guernsey raid was singularly bloodless, and in general unimpressive. 'Let there be no more Guernseys' said Churchill when he heard of its outcome. It was not quite as simple as that. The Navy, despite inadequate landing craft, played its part with the efficiency and sang-froid that one normally attributes to that unparalleled service. The soldiers lacked an enemy to shoot at, but otherwise played their part. In war lessons are learned and re-learned in odd ways. The survivors of Guernsey went on to greater things.

It was unfortunate that for lack of targets and proper landing craft a false impression of the potential of raiding should so soon have reached the mind of the Prime Minister, the Commandos' greatest supporter.

Two days later Admiral of the Fleet Sir Roger Keyes became Director of Combined Operations. The 68-year-old hero of Gallipoli and Zeebrugge was not the man to break windows with guineas.

Lofoten and Spitzbergen

'After fifteen months experience as Director of Combined Operations, and having been frustrated in every worthwhile offensive action I have tried to undertake, I must fully endorse the Prime Minister's comments on the strength of the negative power which controls the war machine in Whitehall . . . Great leaders of the past have always emphasized the value of time in war . . . time is passing and so long as procrastination, the thief of time, is the key-word of the war machine in Whitehall, we shall continue to lose one opportunity after another during the lifetime of opportunities.'

In October 1941 Sir Roger Keyes, who had seldom seen eye to eye with the Cabinet of the Chiefs of Staff, was replaced. His parting salvo, quoted above, was fired in the House of Commons and everyone serving in the Commandos in October 1941 heartily agreed with every word he said. For most of them their months in the Commandos seemed in retrospect to have been one long story of hope deferred. In the early days, during that glorious summer when invasion still threatened England, they had been happy enough. Most of the officers had gone to Lochailort in the Western Highlands where they had been instructed in sophisticated methods of slaughter, and in the art of living off the country. Troops had trained hard in the endeavour to achieve not only perfection but originality; to get away from the tactical legacy of 1914-18 and trench warfare.

In the fall of 1940 five of the Commandos and many assault ships had been concentrated at Inveraray, in preparation for a big operation, the capture of the Azores, which after seemingly endless exercises was cancelled. Next Sir Roger selected Pantelleria as his objective and concentrated his force in the Isle of Arran. This scheme was also cancelled and it cannot be denied that this had an adverse effect on the morale and discipline of at least some troops, but the commander of the Special Service Brigade, Brigadier J C Haydon, DSO, was ready with exhortations adequate to the occasion, and was soon able to revive the original sense of purpose:

'A great enthusiasm at the beginning has evaporated, or at least decreased, owing to the repeated postponements of expected events and enterprises. There is a growing irritation with life . . . this is due partly to these postponements and partly to being harried from pillar to post, on to ships and off them, into billets and out of them, and so on. There is, in short, a sense of frustration.'

The remedy lay with the officers, the best of whom bent all their ingenuity and enthusiasm to devising fresh exercises, tests and techniques, so as to perfect the battle-craft of their men.

In reviving the spirit of his brigade Haydon was helped by three factors. The first was the departure for the Middle East of 'Layforce', whose exploits will be described in the next chapter. The second was the re-organization of the Commandos into a headquarters and six troops, instead of ten. Since this meant that each unit would now have twelve fewer officers, commanding officers had a fairly painless way of getting rid of some of their misfits. The new organization was very much handier from the tactical point of view. Each troop was now to consist of three officers and sixty-two other ranks.

The third factor was the first Lofoten Islands raid. On 21st February the troops embarked at Gourock in the infantry landing ships *Queen Emma* and *Princess Beatrix*, converted cross-Channel steamers. That evening they sailed for Scapa Flow, which was reached next day. A week was spent putting the finishing touches to the planning and training and on 1st March came the signal 'Carry out Operation Claymore'. At midnight the force sailed for Skaalefjord in the Faroe Islands, arriving at 1900 hours on the 2nd. There the five escorting destroyers refuelled and five hours later the expedition sailed again, entering the Westfjord on the night of 3rd March. By 0400 hours next morning the many navigation lights in the vicinity of the Lofotens could be clearly seen. There had been no sign of an enemy. Everything was going

Admiral of the Fleet Sir Roger Keyes

Left, above and below: Crossing obstacles in training. *Below:* Major-General J C Haydon (then Major) the man who trained the Commandos. *Bottom:* HMS Queen Emma, an infantry assault ship with an LCA at the davits

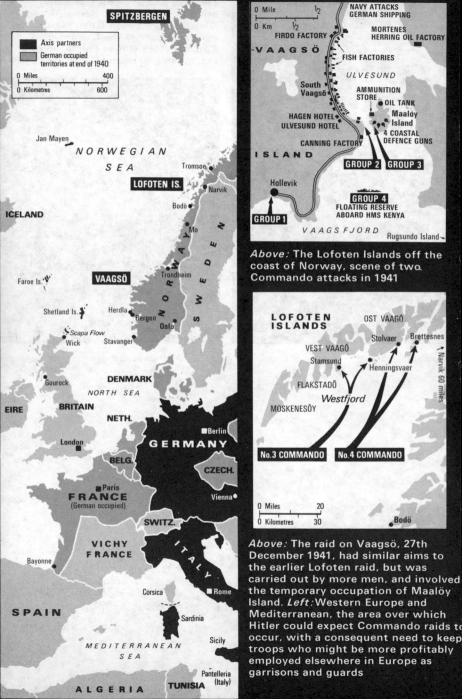

SPITZBERGEN

Axis partners

German occupied territories at end of 1940

0 Miles 400
0 Kilometres 600

NAVY ATTACKS
GERMAN SHIPPING

0 Mile ½
0 Km ½
FIRDO FACTORY

MORTENES
HERRING OIL FACTORY

VAAGSÖ

FISH FACTORIES

South
Vaagsö

ULVESUND

AMMUNITION
STORE

OIL TANK

Maalöy
Island

HAGEN HOTEL
ULVESUND HOTEL

4 COASTAL
DEFENCE GUNS

CANNING FACTORY

ISLAND

Hollevik

GROUP 2   GROUP 3

GROUP 1

GROUP 4
FLOATING RESERVE
ABOARD HMS KENYA

VAAGS FJORD

Rugsundo Island

Above: The Lofoten Islands off the coast of Norway, scene of two Commando attacks in 1941

Jan Mayen

NORWEGIAN SEA

Tromsoe

LOFOTEN IS.

Narvik

ICELAND

Bodö

Mo

Faroe Is.

VAAGSÖ

Trondheim

Shetland Is.

Herdla

Bergen

Scapa Flow

Oslo

Wick

Stavanger

Gourock

DENMARK

NORTH SEA

EIRE

BRITAIN

NETH.

■Berlin

London

GERMANY

BELG.

CZECH.

■Paris

FRANCE
(German occupied)

Vienna●

SWITZ.

**VICHY
FRANCE**

Bayonne

ITALY

Corsica

■Rome

SPAIN

Sardinia

*MEDITERRANEAN
SEA*

Sicily

Pantelleria
(Italy)

ALGERIA   **TUNISIA**

**LOFOTEN
ISLANDS**

OST VAAGÖ

Stolvaer   Brettesnes

VEST VAAGÖ

Stamsund

Henningsvaer

Narvik 60 miles

FLAKSTADÖ

Westfjord

MOSKENESÖY

No.3 COMMANDO   No.4 COMMANDO

0 Miles 20
0 Kilometres 30

Bodö

Above: The raid on Vaagsö, 27th December 1941, had similar aims to the earlier Lofoten raid, but was carried out by more men, and involved the temporary occupation of Maalöy Island. *Left:* Western Europe and Mediterranean, the area over which Hitler could expect Commando raids to occur, with a consequent need to keep troops who might be more profitably employed elsewhere in Europe as garrisons and guards

to plan. This perfect landfall was assisted by the submarine *Sunfish*, which acted as a navigational beacon.

Away to the southward a powerful covering force under no less a person than the Commander-in-Chief, Home Fleet, was hoping that some major German warship would have the temerity to interfere with the proceedings. This force included HMS *Nelson*, *King George V*, *Nigeria*, *Dido* and five destroyers.

The objects of the raid were to destroy fish-oil factories so as to deprive the Germans of glycerine for the manufacture of explosives; to sink enemy shipping; to enlist volunteers for the Norwegian forces in the United Kingdom, and to capture supporters of the traitor, Vidkun Quisling. The ports of Stamsund and Henningsvaer were allotted to Number 3 Commando; Svolvaer and Brettesnes to Number 4. The military force was under the

command of Brigadier Haydon. Detachments of the Royal Engineers and of Norwegian soldiers were with each Commando.

Needless to say officers and men had eagerly devoured every scrap of available information, for few indeed had even so much as heard of the Lofoten Islands previously. The nearest big German garrison was sixty miles away at Bodo, while there was another at Narvik, a distance of one hundred miles. There were posts of twenty men in some of the islands, but none were reported at Stamsund or Svolvaer. A U-Boat had been seen in Narvik in January, but, though armed trawlers escorted the coastal convoys, no other warships were known to be in the area. There were usually some German soldiers aboard the mail steamer which was thought to visit the islands daily.

In March the airfields as far south as Trondheim, 300 miles away, were unfit for aircraft not fitted with skis, and so, for once, the threat from the

The Lofoten Islands raid

Luftwaffe was not a major factor – a considerable luxury at that stage of the war!

Soon after 0600 hours the landing craft began their run in. The sun rose bright as they headed for the snow-clad islands, but the air was chill and the blunt-nosed landing craft slapping the choppy sea sent icy spray over the soldiers. One officer whose 'uniform' included two vests, two pull-overs, a shirt, a waistcoat, and a wool-lined mackintosh and fur-lined boots complained afterwards: 'I was still cold'.

As Durnford-Slater, well ahead in Number 3 Commando's leading craft, approached Stamsund he met a Norwegian fishing fleet coming out. '*Hvor ar Tuska?*' ('Where are the Germans?'), the officers shouted and were somewhat crestfallen to have it confirmed that there were none. The Norwegians for their part hoisted the national colours, which had been flying at half-mast, to the masthead.

The landing at Stamsund proved something of an anti-climax. The 'gently shelving beach' turned out to be a high quay, and the stormers found themselves hauled bodily ashore by the inhabitants who had flocked down to greet them, tying up the landing craft and handing the weapons ashore. After this somewhat un-military beginning the Commando fanned out and lost no time in seizing its objectives. Then the work of destruction began.

The only opposition came from the German armed trawler *Krebbs* which very gallantly took on the destroyer HMS *Somali*, but was set on fire and compelled to surrender.

The results of the raid were highly satisfactory. The volunteers taken off numbered 315, including eight women and one soldier, who emerged from his home in full Norwegian uniform, rifle in hand, accoutred just as he had been when the fighting ended in 1940. The English manager of Allen and Hanbury's factory was rescued from Henningsvaer. German prisoners, mostly Luftwaffe personnel taken by Number 4 Commando, totalled 216. In addition the Norwegian detachment rounded up some sixty Quislings.

Eleven ships with a total tonnage of more than 20,000 tons were sunk, while one trawler was manned and taken back to England. Eighteen factories were destroyed and it is estimated that 800,000 gallons of oil and petrol were burned. The film of all this taking place was an effective piece of war propaganda at a time when there was no surfeit of Allied successes. The only British casualty is thought to have been an officer who succeeded in shooting himself with his Colt automatic, which he had stuck in a trouser's pocket.

The raid had its lighter side. One sergeant, who had been issued with one hundred Kroner for use in the event of his being left behind and having to make his way to neutral Sweden, could only account for seventy when he returned aboard. It transpired that he had found time to bestow the other thirty on a nubile young Norwegian girl whilst ashore. He was known ever after as 'Thirty Kroner So-and-So', but his name shall not be revealed here.

John Durnford-Slater made a memorable harangue to a number of suspected Quislings before departing. He always spoke in a rather breathless, high-pitched voice. Now, speaking with great rapidity, he said: 'Yeah, well, I don't want to hear any more of this bloody Quisling business. It's no bloody good, I'm telling you. If I hear there's been any more of it, I'll be back again and next time I'll take the whole bloody lot of you. Now clear off'.

Small wonder if they departed looking somewhat bemused. Perhaps they were trying to translate the strange English word 'Quisling-business'.

In 1955 Charley Head, who had been Adjutant of Number 3 Commando, revisited the islands, and learned that the Germans had arrived on 5th March and burned a few houses, but they had not shot any of the inhabitants who had welcomed the Commandos so warmly. On the island of Svolvaer, where Number 4 Commando had landed, stands a memorial to eight of the volunteers who had sailed for England in the *Princess Beatrix*. Seven

Demolition party regard their handiwork

Left: German wounded being transferred to hospital ship.
Right: German prisoners and Quislings

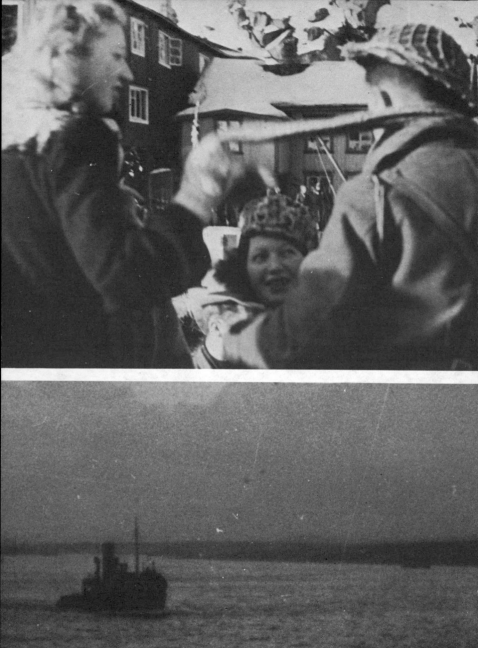

Top left: A fond farewell. *Top right:* Mr Hawes, a Naval officer, and Lieutenant-Colonel Durnford-Slater after the raid. *Above:* The return home.

Spitzbergen

had lost their lives serving with the Royal Navy and one with the Norwegian Troop of Number 10 (Inter-Allied) Commando.

The next important amphibious expedition was not strictly speaking a Commando raid, for the main body of the military force involved was a detachment of Canadian troops under Brigadier A E Potts. Nevertheless it requires mention here as part of the story of Combined Operations. This was the landing in Spitzbergen, 350 miles from the northern point of Norway. The object was to disable the coal mines in order to deny their produce to the Germans.

Once again there was no opposition. The inhabitants were evacuated, the Russians to the USSR, and the Norwegians to the United Kingdom. 450,000 tons of coal were set on fire as well as 275,000 gallons of fuel oil, petrol and grease.

The Germans only learned of the raid when the force was on its way home. On the night 3rd/4th September the wireless station at Tromsoe could be heard trying to get Spitzbergen on the air – in vain.

The Spitzbergen Raid. *Below:* **Canadian Soldiers outside the Communal building.** *Right:* **Fuel dumps on fire at Barentsberg**

This was the last large-scale operation of the period when Sir Roger Keyes was Director of Combined Operations. There were a few minor raids on the French coast, carried out by men of Numbers 2, 5, 9 and 12 Commandos, but it cannot be claimed that any of them did any damage worthy of Hitler's notice. In war the mind of the enemy commander is the ultimate objective and any raiding that had taken place so far had attracted his attention to his Norwegian rather than his French front. For various reasons, including the range of fighter cover, the coasts of Denmark, Germany, Holland and Belgium were not really vulnerable to raiding.

On 27th October 1941 the Lord Louis Mountbatten, GCVO, DSO, ADC, succeeded Sir Roger Keyes as Director of Combined Operations. He was promoted Commodore, First Class. It was a brilliant choice, for which the credit is due to Winston Churchill himself. Mountbatten was a man of forty-one. He had made a tremendous name for himself in command of the destroyer *Kelly*, which, after a splendid fighting career had been sunk off Crete earlier in the year.

H St George Saunders wrote in 'The Green Beret': 'The successor of Keyes was a man of boundless energy and

Left: **Lord Louis Mountbatten.**
Above: **On the polo field**

determination. Lord Louis Mountbatten, a cousin of the King, had spent all his active life in the Royal Navy. In the twenties he had seemed to those who did not know him to be a good-looking naval officer married to a beautiful and wealthy woman, who concerned himself more with the pleasures of life than with its responsibilities. He owned a flat which was the wonder of Mayfair; he played polo; he frequented all the fashionable resorts; he was a hedonist. Nothing, in fact, was further from the truth. These were but the outward signs of a temperament which led him, as it still does, to embrace life with a wide gesture while at the same time being well aware that cakes and ale are but the trimmings of the banquet. Those who knew him well were impressed by the seriousness of purpose which remains the mainspring of his character . . .

The discerning eye of the Prime Minister had long had him in view. He had energy, brains, and determination of the highest order, all qualities in which a Chief of Combined Operations must excel. To these, as well as to his youth, his vigour, and his frank personality, he owed his appointment.'

Sir Roger Keyes was a fire-eater if ever there was one, and the hero of Zeebrugge was greatly admired by the Commando men, whom he tried to launch against the enemy. Even so he was a remote, almost historic figure. In Mountbatten the Commandos found a leader of their own generation. And in one respect Keyes seems to have been seriously at fault. Frustrated by the Chiefs of Staff and by shortages of weapons and landing craft, he had abandoned the realistic policy of launching frequent small scale raids and had attempted to mount operations on a brigade-group scale. The capture of Pantelleria, on which he set his heart, could have done the Allies no good in the early days of 1941. Had he landed 4,000 Commandos there they would have been scarcely more useful than a similar number incarcerated in a German POW camp. It seems that he thought that if his 4,000 men were idle long enough the 'powers that be' would eventually be stirred to action. As he revealed in his parting shots, he underrated Whitehall's capacity for procrastination.

But a new day was dawning.

The adventures of Layforce

'The Commando soldier ... apt à tout'

In February 1941 a considerable detachment from the Special Service Brigade was sent to the Middle East. It consisted of Numbers 7, 8 and 11 Commandos and sailed in the assault ships HMS *Glenroy*, *Glengyle* and *Glenearn*.

In command was Lieutenant-Colonel R E Laycock and a better choice could not have been made. Bob Laycock was a splendid officer, tough and resolute. As befitted an officer of the Royal Horse Guards he demanded the highest standards of courage, initiative and discipline, and in these respects he himself set an unswerving example. To his great qualities of character and personality must be added a thorough professional equipment. He was one of the few senior officers of the Commandos who had had the benefit of a course at the Staff College. Indeed this qualification had nearly curtailed his raiding career before it had begun. When he left Camberley in 1940 he was supposed to go as Anti-Gas Staff Officer to General Headquarters, Middle East. It was not a role to appeal to a thruster, and being determined to get command of one of the Commandos, he lost no time in finding a substitute. And so it came to pass that when Bob Laycock eventually turned up in the Middle East it was not as a Grade III Staff Officer but as the commander of a formidable brigade.

On arrival two small Commandos, 50 and 52, which had been locally raised and recently amalgamated into one, were added to his command. Layforce now became a brigade of the 6th Division of General Wavell's Army, and the Commandos were renamed. Number 7 became 'A' Battalion; Number 8, 'B'; Number 11, 'C'; and the Combined (Middle East) Commando, 'D'.

Layforce arrived in Egypt at a time when Rommel's first onslaught in the desert had wrested the initiative from the British. The situation was further complicated by the German attack on Yugoslavia on 6th April, which was followed soon after by the invasion of Greece.

Major-General R E Laycock

38

Laycock was eager to prove the worth of his as yet untried units, and in April he was ordered to mount a raid on the port of Bardia, in Cyrenaica, which after being captured during General O'Connor's offensive on 5th January 1941 had recently been retaken by Axis forces. The object was to harass the enemy's lines of communication and to inflict damage on his supplies and war material. One complication was that the port was outside the range of fighter cover.

HMS *Glengyle* with 'A' Battalion Commando aboard set sail on the night 19th/20th April, escorted by the anti-aircraft cruiser HMS *Coventry* and the three Australian destroyers, HMAS *Stuart*, *Voyager* and *Waterhen*. HM Submarine *Triumph* was to take up a position two and a half miles off Bardia, and show a white light as a navigational aid. Unfortunately she was attacked by aircraft during her passage and delayed. The aircraft were British.

Below: **Bardia; a forbidding coastline.**
Bottom: **HMS Glengyle**
Below right: **Major-General Bernard Freyberg VC, the defender of Crete**

Captain Courtney of the Folboat Troop (Special Boat Section) was supposed to show a green light from an offshore islet, but his folboat was wrecked by the heavy swell as he was launching it from *Triumph's* conning tower. Thus the navigational lights which *Glengyle* counted upon did not appear. However she reached the correct position and launched her landing craft at 2235 hours. Owing to trouble with the release gear they began their run in fifteen minutes late, but most of them touched down more or less on time.

There were four beaches. At 'A', the most northerly, the men landed without difficulty, wading ashore in two feet of water. They were joined by the men who were meant to land at 'B'. They had been delayed when their craft stuck in the falls and had joined the flotilla steering for 'A'. The senior army officer pointed out the mistake but his sailor knew better. At 'C' the landing party were late. At 'D', though the approach was narrow and difficult, thirty-five men waded ashore through the swell within ten minutes of the right time

All the landings had been unopposed, and indeed except for two motor-cycle patrols and a couple of lorries there were few enemy about. Men from 'A' beach hurled bombs at these last, but they fell short. An officer moving from one party to another failed to give the countersign when challenged, and was shot and mortally wounded. They discovered a dump of tyres which they set on fire with four incendiary bombs. With this they had to be content, and though it burned fiercely for some hours it was not much of an exploit. Some of the men withdrew to 'B' beach found no landing craft there, and a number were taken prisoner.

The men from 'C' beach damaged a bridge, but their explosives made little impression on the road. Their main objective was a pumping station, but they found it so late that they had no time to demolish it.

The men from 'D' beach found four naval guns. Corporal Baxford and Sapper Angus blew up their breaches with gelignite.

The compasses in the assault landing craft proved defective, which complicated the withdrawal, but the *Glen-* *gyle* got back safely to Alexandria at 2300 hours on the 30th.

The raid was a disappointment. The men, most of whom had not been in action before, had moved far too slowly. This was partly because they were afraid of making too much noise, and partly because they tended to take cover as soon as anyone opened fire. More experienced troops might have known that fast moving men are not much of a target in the dark. But if Laycock was ill-content with this performance the Germans were sufficiently alarmed to pull back an armoured brigade from Sollum.

Further raids on Rommel's communications might have paid dividends, but the enemy air force now had the upper hand, and no warship slower than a destroyer could have carried out a raid with any chance of survival. Moreover so many troops had been sent to Greece that Layforce was now practically Wavell's only general reserve. Number 11 Commando had to be sent to Cyprus whose garrison seemed dangerously weak.

By 2nd May the British had been driven out of Greece and eighteen days

later the Germans invaded Crete. The inadequate garrison was commanded by a great fighting soldier, Major-General Freyberg VC, who was determined that his men should give a good account of themselves. For a time the unequal struggle hung in the balance and Layforce was sent as a reinforcement. On 25th May Laycock tried to land at Sphakia but was foiled by bad weather and had to return to Alexandria. Transhipped to the fast minelayer HMS *Abdiel* he returned immediately and managed to land in Suda Bay on the night 26th/27th May. When dawn broke Layforce was holding a defensive position astride the main road inland from Sphakia. Here they were heavily dive-bombed, an ordeal which the men endured with fortitude. Captain Evelyn Waugh, the novelist, an old friend of Bob Laycock's was serving as one of his staff officers. A man of cool, almost insolent courage he delivered himself of this opinion: 'Like all things German it is very efficient, but it goes on much too long.'

By the 28th it was clear that the battle was lost, and that once more the Royal Navy was faced with the task of getting the Army away. It fell to Layforce to cover the retreat. On that day Captain F R J Nicholls led G Troop in a bayonet charge which drove the Germans from a hill enfilading Number 7 Commando's position. It does not fall to everyone to lead a charge with the cold steel. It is an exhilarating experience, as Nicholls revealed when he wrote home a few days later: 'One thing I am certain about after Crete is that, man for man, there is not any question as to who is the better. Although they [the Germans] had every advantage of air support, etc., whenever they counterattacked or got to close quarters, which in our own case was twice, they dropped their weapons and fled before us – a very heartening sight.'

It is sad to have to record that this splendid officer was afterwards killed in Burma.

Laycock, no mean tactician, was not slow to discover the way to fight a rearguard action in the teeth of the Germans. Just before dark he would launch a few light counter attacks, no more than fighting patrols of seven or eight men. This sufficed to keep the Germans quiet for the night – they like their sleep. Even so it was a time of chaos and confusion; a retreat has a nightmare quality that is difficult to describe. Units hard hit and short of officers begin to fall apart, rumour is rife, and an iron hand is needed to keep the sleepy, hungry soldiers from despair. Laycock was equal to the worst the Germans could devise. On the 28th his headquarters, which chanced to have three tanks with it, was ambushed. What followed is best described in his own words: 'By the most fortunate chance the ambush was close to the three tanks and the Germans did not see them. The enemy were about thirty yards or less away from us when my Brigade Major and I jumped into a tank and drove straight over the Germans.'

Thus lightly he dismissed this exploit, but how many brigade commanders in any army can drive a tank at all, let alone leap into one and counterattack on the spur of the moment?

In Crete it needed men of this calibre to keep the men going. The troops of the original garrison were exhausted, footsore and thirsty. The Commando men were no better off. A gallant sergeant, Charles Stewart, recalled that when eventually his men got some rations they ate them 'as quietly as a female pig after suckling her young.' Eventually the Commandos reached the beach at Sphakia only to find that there were hardly any craft to take them off. Stewart, in order to help two wounded comrades, gave up his own chance of escape. One party got back to North Africa under sail in a landing craft, which had run out of fuel. The sail was made of blankets lashed together with bootlaces and the voyage took six days. It is fitting that the name of the Royal Marines, who commanded this unlikely odyssey should be remembered.

The Commando soldier was always ready to turn his hand to anything – *apt a tout* as the old French cavalry put it. All the same they were ill-equipped and too lightly armed for the task they were asked to perform in Crete. If they did their job, and

Reception committee: Stukas dive-bombing British shipping in Suda Bay

The disadvantage of not having air cover. Another view of Suda Bay.

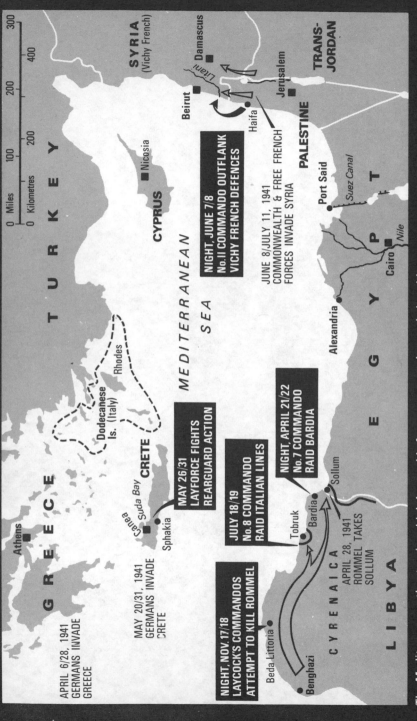

The Mediterranean theatre, in which Laycock's forces operated, mostly in raids behind the German lines in North Africa, although Commandos were used in the defence of Crete and in the invasion of Vichy Syria.

Map labels:

APRIL 6/28, 1941
GERMANS INVADE
GREECE

MAY 20/31, 1941
GERMANS INVADE
CRETE

MAY 26/31
LAYFORCE FIGHTS
REARGUARD ACTION

JULY 18/19
No. 8 COMMANDO
RAID ITALIAN LINES

NIGHT, NOV. 17/18
LAYCOCK'S COMMANDOS
ATTEMPT TO KILL ROMMEL

NIGHT, APRIL 21/22
No. 7 COMMANDO
RAID BARDIA

APRIL 28, 1941
ROMMEL TAKES
SOLLUM

NIGHT, JUNE 7/8
No. 11 COMMANDO OUTFLANK
VICHY FRENCH DEFENCES

JUNE 8/JULY 11, 1941
COMMONWEALTH & FREE FRENCH
FORCES INVADE SYRIA

GREECE · TURKEY · SYRIA (Vichy French) · Damascus · Litani · Beirut · Jerusalem · PALESTINE · TRANS-JORDAN · Haifa · Port Said · Suez Canal · CYPRUS · Nicosia · MEDITERRANEAN SEA · Athens · Dodecanese Is. (Italy) · Rhodes · CRETE · Suda Bay · Canea · Sphakia · Alexandria · Cairo · Nile · EGYPT · Tobruk · Bardia · Sollum · CYRENAICA · LIBYA · Beda Littoria · Benghazi

0 Miles 100 200 300
0 Kilometres 200 400

they certainly did, it was because, inspired by a determined leader, they rose above their purely physical disadvantages. Their casualties numbered some 600 – three-quarters of the force that had landed at Suda Bay.

On 8th June the British were compelled to invade Syria where General Dentz, the French High Commissioner, had permitted the Italians to establish air bases. Australian troops advancing north from Palestine were held up near the mouth of the Litani River. To unlock this line it was decided to land Number 11 Commando, which it will be recalled had been in Cyprus when the rest of Layforce was in Crete. The objective was a strong redoubt covering the bridge at Kafr Bada, the bulk of whose garrison belonged to the 22nd Algerian *Tirailleurs*.

The Commando embarked at Haifa in HMS *Glengyle*, commanded by Captain C H Petrie, RN. The landing was not likely to be an easy one. In summer the mouth of the Litani River is usually closed, and owing to the lie of the land it is extremely difficult to identify from the sea. Moreover there is usually a good deal of surf along the Syrian coast, which makes a landing practically impossible on most nights of the month. Fortunately Captain Petrie had discovered in Haifa a young officer who had served in the Palestine Police. This was Sub-Lietenant F H Colenut, RNVR, a man of courage and resource, who landed on the night 6th/7th June and reconnoitred the beaches. On the strength of his report it was decided to carry out the operation on the following night, landing the Commando in three groups north of the river so as to take the defenders in flank and rear. The left group was to be commanded by Captain George More; the centre by Lieutenant-Colonel R R H Pedder; and the right by Major Geoffrey Keyes.

It had been full moon on the previous night and so the landing craft, which were launched just before dawn, had to run in with the setting moon behind them and the rising sun ahead. Even so they had an unopposed landing, though Keyes's group was put ashore to the south of the river. Peering through the twilight they saw what seemed to be a body of troops, but it turned out to be a cypress grove; the troops dashed ashore and cleared the beach. After a time Keyes realized that he had been landed on the wrong side of the river. He lost no time in getting in touch with an Australian battalion from whom he borrowed a boat. In this he ferried his men across the Litani, in the teeth of heavy fire. Thus the Commandos found themselves tackling the very obstacle that their landing was intended to outflank. Keyes was an officer of the Scots Greys and his troop had been selected from famous cavalry regiments. Here his 'cavaliers' as he called them suffered severely, but they got across, where the Australians, no mean fighting men, had failed.

Dick Pedder, a man of fiery temper, was quick to deliver a blistering rebuke if something displeased him. His group pushed inland with vigour and was soon in action. He was in the act of giving orders to some of his officers when a rifle shot hit him in the head, killing him instantly. The other officers were all wounded, but RSM Fraser took command and led the men forward to take the local barracks and a number of men who were about to reinforce the key redoubt.

Further north George More's group had attacked the French gun line, taking a number of field guns and howitzers; the Commandos were actually outnumbered by their prisoners.

Nevertheless the 22nd *Tirailleurs* had not thrown up the sponge. They still had the support of 4-inch mortars, and they had recovered from their initial surprise. Things were looking pretty black for the two northernmost groups of 11 Commando, when about midday the gallant Keyes came on the scene. Taking command, he quickly reorganized the men, and by 1300 hours the redoubt was in his hands.

It was a cruel fate that decreed that Number 11 Commando's first action should be fought against Frenchmen, and in this bitter action the unit suffered 123 casualties, about a quarter of its strength. Both Major Keyes and Captain More were awarded the Military Cross.

From March to December 1941 Rommel's forces besieged Tobruk, which was resolutely defended by a garrison of Australians and others under General Morshead. In this defence a small detachment of five officers and seventy other ranks of Number 8 Commando played their part, sharing the dangers and hardships of the siege, the worst of which, according to Sergeant Dickason, was the shortage of beer. Their chief exploit was a well planned raid carried out by Captain Mike Keely of the Devonshire Regiment.

The objective was an Italian strongpoint called the Twin Pimples, two small hills overlooking the forward defensive positions of the 18th Indian Cavalry. Before the raid the Commandos familiarised themselves with the terrain by going out on patrol with the Indian cavalrymen, who were adept at night movement.

The raiding party comprised forty men of Number 8 Commando and a demolition party of Australian sappers. Keely had with him two excellent officers: Captain Philip Dunne (Royal Horse Guards), a skilful and original tactician, who had once been a Member of Parliament, and Lieutenant Jock Lewis (Welsh Guards), who before the war had been a well-known amateur jockey.

Most of Number 8 Commando were Guardsmen, picked for their powerful physique. Half Keely's party were armed with rifle and bayonet, the rest with Tommy guns. All carried hand grenades, and a third of them had groundsheets to use as stretchers. These were rolled up and worn over the shoulder like a bandolier.

They set off, walking briskly, at 2300 hours on the night of 18th July. 'It was like an English summer evening and very pleasant', wrote Philip Dunne. 'We moved in complete silence, being particularly careful not to betray ourselves by coughing. We were all wearing rubber boots. We went through the Italian forward positions and then through their main defensive lines. I shall never know if they were manned or not because we heard nothing from them and were very careful to make no noise.'

They reached the track by which the Italians brought up their rations, turned to the right and got in the rear of the Pimples. As they approached the 18th Cavalry staged a diversion and the Italians began putting up flares and firing at the Indian position.

While the Italians were busily engaged to their front the Commandos were nearing their rear. They were not challenged until they were thirty yards from the position, then they charged in firing from the hip and shouting their password: 'Jock'. The fight only lasted three or four minutes. Keely was seen to charge a machine-gun nest, clouting the crew with the butt of his Tommy gun. According to Sergeant Dickason: 'his Tommy gun was rendered useless, but so were the enemy gunners', The Italians took cover in their dugouts and the Commandos bombed them out with Mills grenades. Before the raiders withdrew the Australian sappers blew up the Italian ammunition dump and some mortars. It was all over inside a quarter of an hour, and at a cost of one man mortally wounded and four others wounded. The raiders were no more than one hundred yards on their way home when the Italian artillery brought down defensive fire and began to plaster the Twin Pimples. In planning the raid it was reckoned that it would take them fifteen minutes to realize what was going on, a nice piece of calculation in a thoroughly well planned and executed operation.

After the Litani river Number 11 Commando had returned to Cyprus, but what remained of the rest of Layforce was concentrated near Alexandria. Replacements for the men lost in Crete and Syria were not forthcoming and it was reluctantly decided to disband the force. Most of the men returned to their units, but a few went with David Stirling, Jock Lewis, and Paddy Mayne to form the Special Air Service, and to write a new chapter in the history of raiding.

A small force, which was designed to wage amphibious warfare in the Mediterranean, remained under Laycock's command. It was with these men that he made his daring attempt to turn the course of the war by eliminating the Desert Fox himself.

Laycock himself was in overall command of the operation while Lieutenant-Colonel Keyes had asked to lead the actual assault on Rommel's Headquarters at Beda Littoria. The objective laid down by the Eighth

Lieutenant-Colonel Geoffrey Keyes VC

Army, under whose operational command the group came, was to kill or capture the German general. The raid was to take place at midnight on 17th/18th November and was to coincide with the opening of General Auchinleck's offensive to relieve Tobruk. It involved landing far behind the enemy lines.

Laycock did not conceal from his followers that he considered the raid extremely hazardous. The attack on Rommel's house, he thought, meant almost certain death for the assault party. Moreover, as he frankly pointed out,'the chances of being evacuated after the operation were very slender.' The soldiers were quite unmoved by these realistic, if gloomy, forebodings, while Keyes for his part urged Laycock not to repeat them lest the 'powers that be' should cancel the whole show.

The force sailed from Alexandria on 10th November in the submarines *Torbay* and *Talisman*. The British soldier loves novelty and the men,

Below: HMS Torbay. *Bottom:* HMS Talisman

delighted at this fresh and relatively subtle way of reaching their target, had nothing but praise for their food and accommodation.

Both submarines reached the rendezvous on time, and a torch flashed from the shore signalled that the beach was clear. Disguised as an Arab, Captain J E Haselden, an intrepid Intelligence officer, had been dropped by the Desert Reconnaissance Group to act as a one-man reception committee. A heavy swell rendered the landing excessively hazardous. As Keyes's party were launching their two-man rubber boats from the *Torbay* a large wave swept four of them into the sea with several of the soldiers. Laycock had even more trouble landing from the *Talisman* and most of his boats were capsized. Only half of the two parties eventually struggled ashore and gained the *wadi* where they were to lie up for the day.

The force was now divided into three groups. Laycock with a sergeant and two men was to stay in the *wadi* to look after the dump of ammunition and rations, and to direct the rest of the *Talisman* party if they got ashore next

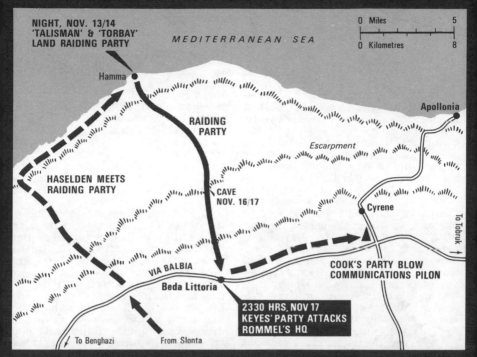

**NIGHT, NOV. 13/14
'TALISMAN' & 'TORBAY'
LAND RAIDING PARTY**

MEDITERRANEAN SEA

0 Miles 5
0 Kilometres 8

Hamma

Apollonia

**RAIDING
PARTY**

Escarpment

**HASELDEN MEETS
RAIDING PARTY**

**CAVE
NOV. 16/17**

Cyrene

To Tobruk

VIA BALBIA

**COOK'S PARTY BLOW
COMMUNICATIONS PILON**

Beda Littoria

**2330 HRS, NOV 17
KEYES' PARTY ATTACKS
ROMMEL'S HQ**

To Benghazi   From Slonta

The courageous but unfortunate attack on Rommel's HQ, the *Rommel-haus*.
There were only two survivors from the raiding party.

night. Lieutenant Gay Cook and six men were to cut the telephone and telegraph wires at the crossroads south of Cyrene. Keyes was to lead the actual assault.

The sun dried the men's clothes as they lay in the *wadi*. Once an aircraft, painted with red crosses, flew over, but evidently they were not spotted. In the afternoon it came on to rain.

At 2000 hours Keyes set off. The going, mostly on rock-strewn sheep tracks, was extremely difficult, but dawn found Keyes and his men ensconced on a small hill. Here they were discovered by a party of Arabs armed with Italian carbines. Fortunately the party included Corporal Drori, a Palestinian who spoke perfect Arabic. With him as interpreter Keyes won over their leader, a 'very villainous-looking Arab with a red headcloth wound round his head at a raffish angle'. (From *The Green Beret* by H St George Saunders). At midday the Arabs brought kid's meat and soup, the first hot meal the men had had for thirty-six hours. Keyes was able to buy them some cigarettes with Italian money he had with him.

When it got dark they set out once more, the 'brigand' leading them in about two and a half hours to a large, dry cave with 'an appalling smell of goat'. Here they rested, moving on next morning, since in the bad weather goatherds were likely to shelter in the cave. Their next hide was a small wood, where wild cyclamen grew. Here they breakfasted on 'arbutus berries that look and taste like strawberries and are called by the Senussi the Fruit of God'. Next Keyes set out on a reconnaissance and was able to make out the escarpments near the objective. A thunderstorm came on and he decided to risk returning to the cover of the cave. An Arab boy, who had accompanied the guide, spied out the land in and around Beda Littoria, and from his information Keyes was able to draw 'an excellent sketch map of the house and its surroundings'. With its aid he was able to brief them for the attack, assigning each group the place where it was to deploy. It was a day of thunderstorms and the desert turned to mud. Keyes, making the best of things, pointed out that in the foul weather their approach march

was the less likely to be observed.

At 1800 hours on the 17th the raiding party set off in pouring rain to march the last stage of their journey. They were soon soaked, but struggling along in the ankle-deep mud, they had reached the foot of the rocky escarpment by 2230 hours. They had time for a short rest before scaling this obstacle. There was a bad moment half-way up, when they 'roused a watchdog and a stream of light issued from the door of a hut . . . a hundred yards on our flank. As we crouched motionless, hardly breathing, we heard a man shouting at the dog. Finally the door closed'.

They found the track which according to their Arab guides led to the back of Rommel's Headquarters. Here Cook's party set off to carry out its task. The rest began their final approach, Keyes himself and Sergeant Terry acting as scouts and Captain Campbell bringing up the main body fifty yards behind them. When they had gone a quarter of a mile they dropped the guides, impressing upon them that they must await the raiders' return or forfeit their reward. Pushing on, weapons at the ready, at about 2330 hours they reached some outbuildings within one hundred yards of the headquarters house. While Keyes and Terry were making their final reconnaissance a dog began to bark, and an Italian soldier accompanied by an Arab came out of a hut. Campbell told him in German – 'as imperiously as I could' – that they were a German patrol, an assertion which Corporal Drori repeated in Italian. As the soldier turned away Keyes returned, and deployed his men for the assault. Keyes, supported by Campbell and Terry, pushed through a hedge into the garden, round a corner, and was running up a flight of steps to some glass-topped doors when a German officer, in steel helmet and greatcoat, appeared in his path. Campbell describes what followed:

'Geoffrey at once closed with him, covering him with his Tommy gun. The man seized the muzzle of Geoffrey's gun and tried to wrest it from him. Before I or Terry could get round behind him he retreated, still holding on to Geoffrey, to a position with his back to the wall and his

Right: Sergeant J Terry. *Below:* The house in Beda Littoria

German and Italian soldiers at Keyes's funeral

either side protected by the first and second pair of doors at the entrance. Geoffrey could not draw a knife and neither I nor Terry could get round Geoffrey as the doors were in the way, so I shot the man with my .38 revolver which I knew would make less noise than Geoffrey's Tommy gun. Geoffrey then gave the order to use Tommy guns and grenades, since we had to presume that my revolver shot had been heard. We found ourselves in a large hall with a stone floor and stone stairway leading to the upper stories, and with a number of doors opening out of the hall which was very dimly lit. We heard a man in heavy boots clattering down the stairs. As he came to the turn and his feet came in sight, Sergeant Terry fired a burst with his Tommy gun. The man turned and fled away upstairs'.

Keyes threw open a door, but the room was empty. Then, pointing to a light shining under the next door, he flung it open. Inside were something like ten Germans in steel helmets, sitting and standing. Campbell goes on: 'Geoffrey fired two or three rounds

with his Colt .45 automatic, and I said: "Wait, I'll throw a grenade in".' Keyes slammed the door shut and held it while Campbell pulled the pin out. 'I said "Right," and Geoffrey opened the door and I threw in the grenade which I saw roll to the middle of the room. "Well Done," said Keyes. A German fired and hit Geoffrey just above the heart'.

He fell unconscious. Campbell shut the door and instantly his grenade 'burst with a shattering explosion'. The light in the room went out, and there was complete silence. Campbell and Terry carried Keyes outside and laid him on the grass by the steps. 'He must have died as we were carrying him outside, for when I felt his heart it had ceased to beat'.

Campbell went back through the hall of the building, and then round to the back entrance, where a Commando soldier took him for a German and shot him. He was badly wounded in the leg. When the soldiers said they would carry him back to the beach, a distance of twenty-five miles, he ordered them to leave him, and it fell to Keyes's devoted follower, Sergeant Terry, to conduct the withdrawal. Soon afterwards the Germans found

Campbell and took him to hospital. His leg had to be amputated. The Germans chivalrously accorded Keyes full military honours, and the chaplain of the garrison church at Potsdam conducted the service. For his determined, gallant and skilful leadership in this desperate enterprise he was awarded the Victoria Cross. He had proved himself a worthy son of a fire-eating father.

Ironically enough it proved that Rommel had never lived in the house attacked, which was in fact the headquarters of German and Italian supply services. Rommel himself was nowhere near, for he was in the forward area with his troops.

Terry succeeded in leading the raiders back to Laycock in the *wadi*, but they waited in vain for Cook. It transpired subsequently that he carried out his mission, but had fallen into the hands of the enemy on the way back.

The *Torbay* returned on the night of the 20th and flashed a message in morse, which Laycock could read, saying that the sea was too rough and she would return the next night. A rubber dinghy with food and water was floated ashore.

Laycock concealed his men in caves with standing patrols watching the flanks. At noon the post to the west was engaged by Arab levies of the Italians. He sent two small parties to outflank these assailants, but some Germans arrived to support the levies, and foiled this move. Pryor, the commander of one of them, was severely wounded, but managed to crawl back. A large party of Italians appeared on the skyline a mile to the north. They did nothing, but by 1400 hours the Germans, keeping up a heavy fire, had closed to within 200 yards of the caves. Laycock now broke his force up into small parties and ordered them to dash across the open and take cover among the hills inland. They were to try and get in touch with the *Talisman*, or to hide in the *wadis* until our own forces should overrun the area. Pryor was left behind with a medical orderly. He was captured and led off on a mule watched 'by a lovely red-backed shrike sitting on a juniper bush.' (From *The Green Beret* by H St George Saunders.)

Bob Laycock and Sergeant Terry ran the gauntlet of continual sniping till they reached the thick scrub of the Jebel. Then they set out to join the Eighth Army. The Arabs befriended them, conversing in broken Italian. 'For instance, a Senussi, holding up his five fingers, pointing at us and then drawing his fore-finger across his throat, meant that five of our original raiding party had been murdered by the Arabs and handed over to the Germans'. Sometimes they had to live for as much as two and a half days on berries alone, but though weakened by lack of food, they never lacked water for it rained continuously.

On Christmas Day 1941, forty-one days after they had set out on the raid, they reached the British forces at Cyrene – the only two to get back. 'On joining them we fell upon the marmalade offered to us and polished off a pot each'.

Colonel Laycock flew back to Cairo to report. There he heard that Haydon was to become military adviser to Mountbatten. He was to return to England and take command of the Special Service Brigade.

Vaagso

'Norway is the zone of destiny in this war. I demand unconditional obedience to my commands and directives concerning the defence of this area.' Adolf Hitler January 1942.

With Mountbatten at the helm a new sense of urgency began to pervade the whole Combined Operations organization, for he soon demonstrated a truly remarkable skill in cutting through red-tape. and oiling the wheels of inter-Service cooperation. It took him precisely two months to lay on his first big raid, an operation which was to have a subtle influence on the whole future course of the war. Vaagso was, moreoever, a minor classic of amphibious warfare, a raid which, despite the multitudinous accidents inseparable from warfare, actually went according to plan, in that all the groups into which the force was divided carried out their assigned tasks.

In general the object of the raid was to attack and destroy the German garrison in the little Norwegian port of South Vaagso. From the strategic point of view this was part of the British policy of harassing the Germans. The more troops they employed to defend the coasts of northwest Europe the less they would have to fight in Russia or North Africa. From the tactical point of view the intention was to destroy the garrison, blow up the fish-oil factories, sink shipping. bring Norwegian volunteers to Britain, capture code-books and documents. and round up Quislings.

The garrison was thought to consist of 150 infantry, a tank and one hundred men of the Labour Corps. A four-gun battery on the islet of Maaloy covered Vaags Fjord, as did a two-gun battery on Rugsundo Island, which last was not one of the objectives. There was a mobile battery of 105mm guns at Halsor on the north coast of Vaagso Island, covering the northern entrance to Ulvesund, where German convoys used to form up, and where shipping could be expected, including armed trawlers. The Germans had no other warships in the area.

The Luftwaffe had three airfields in

Central Norway, which were within range of Vaagso. They were Herdla, Stavanger, and Trondheim. Fighters (Me 109s) from the last two would have to refuel at Herdla if they were to operate over Vaagso.

The joint force commanders were appointed on 6th December. They were Rear-Admiral H M Burrough, CB, and Brigadier J C Haydon. Their headquarters ship was the 6 inch cruiser HMS *Kenya*. The force was to be escorted and supported by four warships from the 17th destroyer flotilla, HMS *Onslow, Oribi, Offa* and *Chiddingfold*. The soldiers were to be landed from the infantry assault ships HMS *Prince Charles* and *Prince Leopold*. HM Submarine *Tuna* was to play the part of navigational beacon, a point of great importance for earlier in the month a raid on Floro, twenty-five miles south of Vaagso, had been foiled simply because the naval commander was uncertain of his landfall.

The force detailed for the landing consisted of fifty-one officers and 525 other ranks under the command of Lieutenant-Colonel J F Durnford-Slater (Number 3 Commando). It consisted of Number 3 Commando; a troop and a half of Number 2 Commando; detachments of Royal Engineers (Number 6 Commando); Royal Army Medical Corps (Number 4 Commando); and Intelligence officers from the War Office and a Press Unit. Men of the Royal Norwegian Army were attached as guides and interpreters.

The Royal Air Force had only two fighter bases within operational range of Vaagso. These were Sumburgh in the Shetland Islands and Wick at the extreme north of Scotland. They were respectively 250 and 400 nautical miles from Vaagso. From these bases the Beaufighters and Blenheim fighters of Numbers 235, 236, 248, 254 and 404 squadrons would just be able to give the expedition a measure of fighter cover. Bombing missions were assigned to Hampdens of 50 Squadron and Blenheim bombers of 110 and 114 Squadrons of Coastal Command.

On 13th December Number 3 Commando embarked and sailed for Scapa, where the raiding force assembled and the final exercises took place. The briefing was as thorough as man could make it. With maps, air photo-

graphs and models every single ma was shown his task and a variety c possible alternatives: every man wa to be sure he understood his role.

Lord Louis Mountbatten appeare for a last minute visit. His pep tal to the assembled troops ended: 'On last thing. When my ship, the des troyer *Kelly*, went down off Cret earlier this year the German machine-gunned the survivors in th water. There's absolutely no need t treat them gently on my account Good luck to you all!'

The men were wildly enthusiastic and at least one troop commande felt it necessary to impress on hi men the need to take prisoners accord ing to the normal usages of war. Bu though most of them had been a Dunkirk, he need not have worried brutality and bravery seldom g hand in hand.

At 2115 hours on Christmas Ev the force sailed for Sollum Voe i the Shetlands. A westerly gale, Forc 8, was coming in from the Atlantic and the assault ships with all thei top hamper of landing craft wer rolling as if they meant to turn turtle The force reached Sollum Voe, some what battered, at 1300 hours on Christ mas Day, and the repair parties se to work. *Prince Charles* had shippe about 120 tons of water, and fou cabins on C deck had been flooded *Chiddingfold* was ordered alongside t help her pump out.

The storm had not yet blown itsel out, and according to the weathe forecast it would be another twelv or eighteen hours before it did so In view of this and the damage alread sustained, Admiral Burrough decide to postpone the raid for twenty-fou hours. The Commandos, all too use to operations that got cancelled a the last moment, speculated endlessl as to the reason for this delay Rumours were rife, perhaps the mos imaginative being that the Pop would not like it if there were opera tions on Christmas Day. And s Captain Butziger's gunners, celebrat ing round the Christmas tree wit which they had decorated one of thei barrack huts, got a day's grace.

Next day Number 6 Command

Above: HMS Kenya. *Below:* HMS Tun

Pep talk. Lord Louis Mountbatten with soldiers of No 3 Commando before the Vaagso raid

went ashore far to the north at Reine in the Lofoten Islands, an operation which served to some extent to divert the German attention from the more damaging blow that was about to fall on their forces in Central Norway.

At 1600 hours on 26th December the force sailed once more, and with a following sea, but a falling wind, began the last 300 miles of its voyage.

It was still dark as the troops mustered at their boat stations, every man wearing a leather jerkin or a roll-neck sweater in addition to his normal attire. It was bitterly cold. As it grew light the snowclad land ahead could be seen rising sheer out of the sea, with here and there a light twinkling from the few scattered houses. The silent ships steaming towards this rugged shore made a scene of breathtaking beauty. To Captain Michael Denny, Burrough's flag captain, it must have seemed particularly lovely, for he had made a perfect landfall. *Kenya's* asdic received a signal from *Tuna*, whose conning tower was sighted within one minute of the pre-arranged time. As the flotilla made for the entrance of the fjord, clearing Klovning Island and the Skarningerne rocks, Hampdens began to fly in from the west.

'It was a very eerie sensation entering the fjord in absolute silence and very slowly,' wrote Major Robert Henriques, the well-known author, who was serving as Haydon's brigade major. 'I wondered what was going to happen, for it seemed that the ship (HMS *Kenya*) had lost her proper element, that she was no longer a free ship at sea. Occasionally I saw a little hut with a light burning in it and I wondered whether the light would be suddenly switched off, which would mean that the enemy had spotted us, or whether it would continue to burn as some Norwegian fisherman got out of bed, stretched himself and went off to his nets.

'As we entered the fjord the naval commander gave the order "Hoist the battle ensign!" By tradition the navy then hands down its normal white ensign and replaces it with a thing the size of a double sheet to give the enemy something to shoot at'.

As the landing-craft were lowered the Hampdens attacked Rugsundo

and the soldiers could see the distant tracer mount slowly, and against the dark dawn sky. Suddenly the *Chiddingfold* fired an accidental burst from a Bofors. 'That's given the position away,' muttered the pessimist who is inevitably to be found in even the best of units. At 08.42 hours the landing-craft began to move, up the fjord.

For the German garrison the day's work had already begun. The programme for the men of the infantry platoon in South Vaagso was work on their defensive position at the south end of the town, thus by chance they were already at their alarm post. In a hut on Maaloy an NCO was giving the personnel of the battery a lecture on military courtesy: 'How to behave in the presence of an officer'. Captain Butziger had not yet put in an appearance: he was having a shave. His orderly was cleaning his boots. The telephone rang but he was a man who put first things first: he went on with his polishing. Unable to get any response from the battery the lookout at Husevaagso rang through to the harbour captain's office in South Vaagso, and reported that he had seen what appeared to be seven blacked-out destroyers entering the fjord. A clerk assured him that all was well.

'We are expecting a small convoy this morning. It seems they are a little ahead of schedule'.

'They don't look like merchant ships to me,' the lookout replied, only to be crushed with the suggestion that he was still celebrating Christmas! 'Take care you don't get found drunk on duty!'

So far from being tight, the lookout was a conscientious individual and not lacking in persistence. 'Unidentified warships entering fjord' he wrote on a piece of paper, and handed it to the signal orderly to send by blinker lamp to the naval signal station at Maaloy. The recipient, one Van Soest, does not seem to have been quite so cool as the lookout. He acknowledged the message but then, instead of alerting Butziger, who was not more than 200 yards from him, jumped into a boat and rowed across to tell Leutnant zur See Sebelin, the harbourmaster at South

Vaagso. And all this time the British were coming nearer and nearer.

Soon the last two landing-craft of the port column turned away to run in and land at Hollevik, where there was known to be a German post. Minutes passed. Maaloy hove in sight and on the bridge of HMS *Kenya* Admiral Burrough gave the order. 'Open the line of fire.' It was 08.48 hours.

In the Hagen Hotel, his headquarters, Leutnant Sebelin listened to Van Soest's story.

'Did you notify the battery?'

'No, sir. After all, they are an army battery. This is a naval signal'.

Before Sebelin had time to comment there was a crash and *Kenya's* first salvo landed in the town. Thereafter she was on target, and in the next nine minutes she put something like 450 6-inch shells into an area of 250 square yards. The soldiers in the landing-craft could see pieces of the barrack huts flying through the air. *Onslow* and *Offa* lost no time in adding their contribution. The German infantry in Vaagso jumped into their trenches and wondered when it would be their turn. Out in the fjord they could see two columns of landing-craft moving steadily towards Maaloy at about six knots.

The Commandos in their LCA were wondering how long it would be before the four guns on Maaloy, which they were nearing head-on in a kind of amphibious 'Charge of the Light Brigade', would open up on them. They need not have worried. The covering fire from *Kenya* was more than enough to keep Butziger and most of his men in their bunker.

At 08.57 hours Durnford-Slater in the leading craft of the port column put up ten red Verey lights and as the Hampdens came in to drop smoke bombs on the landing places, *Kenya* ceased fire. There came a sudden calm broken only by a few bursts of light machine gun fire and the skirling of Major Jack Churchill's bagpipes. Standing erect in the leading craft of the starboard column he was playing 'The March of the Cameron Men'.

Durnford-Slater had divided his command into five main groups. The first group, of about fifty men,

under Lieutenant R Clement, was to clear Hollevik and act as a reserve. The second group, of about 200 men under Durnford-Slater himself, was to take South Vaagso. The third group, of 105 men under Major Churchill, was to take Maaloy and demolish the Mortenes factory. The fourth group, with sixty-five men under Captain R H Hooper, was to act as a floating reserve in HMS *Kenya*. Lastly, the fifth group, thirty men under Captain D Birney, was to block the road at Rodberg.

Lieutenant Clement carried out his task almost without opposition. The two German marines found at Hollevik were both badly wounded and captured. The other eight men from the post had gone to Vaagso for breakfast. Clement attempted to report the position to Commando HQ by wireless, but failing to make contact, signalled his message to *Kenya* so that it could be relayed to Durnford-Slater, who gave instructions for Clement to move up the coast road and come into reserve in South Vaagso.

By this time group 2 could do with reinforcements. Even as it ran in it was hard hit, not by the infantry dug in near the landing place, but by the second of the Hampdens, which were dropping smoke bombs. The German armed trawler *Fohn*, lying in Ulvesund, hit one engine with a burst of anti-aircraft fire. Seconds later the bombardier released a 60 pound phosporus smoke-bomb which by a strange and most unlikely mischance fell in Lieutenant Arthur Komrower's landing-craft, killing or burning nearly half of 1 Troop. Komrower, himself leaping ashore, was trapped half under the landing craft, which was crushing his leg. The Norwegian captain, Martin Linge, dashed into the icy water and rescued him.

The rest of group 2 surged ashore under the cover of a low cliff. They were soon in action. Lieutenant Bill Lloyd, a swarthy Australian, 'bushwhacked' a section of Germans as they ran forward to man their alarm post. With bullets whining overhead 3 and 4 troops rushed in among the wooden houses and factories of Vaagso. Here they were met by German infantry, who for the most part had

Below: HMS Onslow. *Bottom:* HMS Oribi. *Top right:* A flotilla of lightly armoured assault landing craft. They were designed to carry approximately 35 men with their equipment. *Bottom right:* A destroyer passes between Vaagso and Maaloy

Above: Bren-gunner aboard an LCA heads for Vaagso. The church is in the background. *Left:* The only 3-inch mortar in action. *Right:* Covering fire from a Bren

Left: Captain Algy Forester. *Below:* Fighting in the streets

seen action in the Norwegian campaign of 1940, and fought with tenacity. When Oberleutnant Bremer fell defending his strongpoint, Stabsfeldwebel Lebrenz took over command. In the midst of a hostile population every single German bore a hand. The unit chaplain was among the first to fall. Leutnant Sebelin lost no time in getting a grip on the headquarters personnel and sailors, so as to give the defence a bit of depth.

After about a quarter of an hour's fighting Captain Giles (3 Troop) moving up on the left ran into a large house which the German infantry had turned into a strongpoint. Sniped from the windows his men worked slowly forward, firing short bursts, and dashing across the snow-covered gaps to take cover behind buildings, until at length they were close enough to rush the building. Then Giles, a man of gigantic stature, led a wild charge, they burst through the front door, and stormed through the house hurling grenades into each door they came to. The surviving Germans fled through the back door followed by Giles, who stood an instant silhouetted as he glanced each way to decide his next move. A lurking rifleman shot him at close range, and he died almost at once. About the same time his senior subaltern, Lieutenant Mike Hall, had his left elbow shattered by a bullet and 3 Troop's assault began to run out of steam.

On the right Captain Algy Forrester, a fire-eater who had served in Norway in 1940, led his depleted 4 Troop straight up the main street, throwing grenades into the houses, and firing from the hip with his Tommy gun. 'I shouldn't have liked to have been a German in his path,' was Durnford-Slater's comment. Forrester was a host in himself. He needed to be, for Komrower, valiantly hobbling to his support, had hardly any of his section in action, and the ardent Lloyd, soon after his initial success, had been shot through the neck and dangerously wounded. Meanwhile Sebelin had got a handful of men together and improvised a strongpoint in and around the Ulvesund Hotel. By the time 4 Troop came on the scene the Germans were in position. The place could only be carried by a frontal assault. Forrester pulled the pin from a grenade and dashed for the front door. A German inside fired and he fell forwards, his grenade bursting beneath him. Now the only officer left was the Norwegian, Martin Linge, whose task was to collect such secret documents as he could from the German headquarters. Without hesitation he assumed command of 4 Troop. The men knew him well enough to recognize a real leader, and they followed him in a second assault. As he dashed round the corner of a building, a bullet pierced his chest and he fell dead almost in the doorway of the hotel. And so the second attack on the Ulvesund Hotel ebbed away.

4 Troop now seemed to be practically leaderless, but the hour found the man, one 'Knocker' White of the Queen's Own Royal West Kent Regiment. Although a solider with considerable experience he was only a full corporal, and there were certainly those present who outranked him. But while the loss of their officers had numbed some of the NCOs, in White it had merely stoked up a sort of fighting fury. Finding that nobody else was doing anything positive he began to rap out an order or two, and finding himself being unquestioningly obeyed, he took charge.

It chanced that Number 1 Troop, thanks to a piece of private enterprise on the part of Captain Bill Bradley, possessed a 3 inch mortar. It cannot be claimed that its crew were well drilled, but though they shrank back and covered their ears every time it went off, they could at least fire it. Sergeant Ramsey now appeared and brought this piece into action at a range that cannot have exceeded one hundred yards. Its first bomb seems to have gone down a chimney in the enemy strongpoint, and is said to have caused thirteen casualties. This lucky shot probably turned the course of the fight. At any rate Corporal White with the survivors of 4 Troop and a handful of Norwegians were able with bomb, Tommy gun and rifle, to overcome the last resistance of the resolutely held but now blazing German strongpoint.

Captain A G Komrower

Back at his command post John Durnford-Slater awaited progress reports with what patience he could muster.

At 1020 hours he sent a signal to *Kenya* reporting that the situation in the northern end of the town was not clear and that he had lost wireless touch with 3 and 4 Troops whose sets had been destroyed. Soon afterwards he followed this with a message: 'Fairly strong opposition being encountered in centre and north end of Vaagso.' He requested that the whole of Group 4 should be sent in on Group 2's original landing place. To this

A blazing German storehouse on Maaloy

Brigadier Haydon consented.

By this time the colonel had probably sent for 2 Troop. He also signalled to Major Churchill to send what men he could spare. This done, at about 1030 hours, he went forward to reconnoitre. His old friend and signals officer took it into his head to accompany him. There was a lot of shooting going on, but Durnford-Slater, pistol in hand, walked briskly up the main street, looking neither to right nor left. Though he had been on the Guernsey and Lofoten raids he had not previously been under fire, but he had been a daring horseman before the war. Racing and pigsticking had developed his robust frame and his

Landing under fire

Below: Advancing up the main street of Vaagso. *Right:* Reserve ammunition is brought up the main street

48206

Spring Branch Senior High School

iron nerve. Charley Heed was not exactly the most timorous of men, although a certain tactical discretion led him to say: 'You keep a lookout for snipers on the left, sir, and I'll take the right.'

'Lookout nothing,' snapped John, 'I'm in a hurry.' He reached the Ulvesund Hotel unscathed.

Group 3 deployed swiftly as their four landing-craft touched the rocky ledge of Maaloy. Major Churchill disappeared, sword in hand, into the thick smoke, uttering warlike cries. No braver man fought at Vaagso that day, a gallant man to follow in action, though decidedly conservative in his military ideas. He is the only man who, to the certain knowledge of the present writer, has transfixed a German with an arrow from a longbow – but that is another story.

The two troops, 5 under Captain Sandy Ronald, and 6 under Captain

Young, negotiated the German wire unopposed. A shell had torn a breach through which 6 Troop passed and nobody trod on a mine. Before the smoke had cleared the empty gun positions had been occupied and white Verey lights were soaring skywards to say 'Here I am'. So far no enemy had shown himself. Now a German soldier appeared, dashing out of the smoke as if heading a counterattack against Number 2 gun site. Three rifle shots rang out. He spun round, screamed, and died. 6 Troop rose and advanced down a slight slope towards the huts. Suddenly a little procession appeared, a German officer and some fifteen unarmed men escorted by Lance-Sergeant George Herbert, MM, and two of his sub-section, Banger Halls and Dick Hughes. This group, fully half the personnel of the battery and its commander Captain Butziger, had been rounded up in the bunker to which they had retired when the first British planes came over.

After this it did not take long to clear the rest of the islet. There was a brief scuffle at the battery office where two Germans were killed, but

On Maaloy Island. *Below:* **German ammunition on fire. Vaagso town in background.** *Right:* **At the landing place, a medical orderly treats a minor casualty**

the capture of the battery took no more than eight minutes. In fact it was taken so quickly that some of 6 Troop were able to swing round one of the guns (they were Belgian 75s), and engage the *Fohn* before she could get out of range, scoring two hits, but with unfused shells.

Perhaps a dozen men of the battery had fallen during the shelling. The crew of the light ack-ack gun had been killed at their piece, but though empty rounds were found in Number 1 gun site nobody seems to have seen it fire at the landing-craft.

Among the captives were two young women, one Belgian and one Norwegian, who might be described as camp followers.

With the island safely in his hands Major Churchill despatched Captain Ronald to Mortenes, where he landed unopposed and destroyed the factory. 6 Troop's demolition squad under Lieutenant Brandwood proceeded to blow up the guns and destroy all the German installations in the island, including a large store of mines which Butziger had not got round to laying.

At about 1015 hours Jack Churchill got a message from the colonel asking for reinforcements. Soon afterwards Captain Young and eighteen of his men landed not far from the northeast corner of the cemetery, where they were met by Charley Head, the signals officer.

The colonel was not far away, standing in the middle of the main street, smiling.

'Well, Peter, I am glad to see you.' Briefly he told 6 Troop's commander of the attacks on the Ulvesund Hotel, of the losses among the officers and the splendid leadership of Corporal White. It was evident that the attack had lost its momentum. Most of 1 Troop was busy with demolitions, but part of 2 Troop had come up under a fiery lieutenant, Denis O'Flaherty. They were clearing warehouses on the waterfront. The floating reserve had been summoned and was coming ashore.

The party from 6 Troop moved off to reinforce the attack along the shores of the fjord. At first all went well. The 2 Troop men had accounted for several Germans, though not without loss to themselves, O'Flaherty himself

Major Jack Churchill examines one of
the four captured Belgian 75s

being nicked in the shoulder.

Four Germans surrendered when men of 6 and 2 Troops rushed a German storehouse. Then the trouble started. Sergeant Hughes and Trooper Clarke were both shot, the former mortally, and nobody could say where the shooting was coming from. Cramped between the storehouse and a woodpile the party had to get room to reorganize. This meant seizing the Red Warehouse sixty yards ahead across a bare patch of snow. Whether the building was occupied none could tell. The troop commander was about half way across the square when a German soldier appeared in the door and began flinging stick grenades. He missed, and his third grenade failed to go off. When about a dozen Mills bombs had been flung into it, an attempt was made to clear the building, but the Germans were still alive. They had retired into an inner room and as the Commandos came through the door fired on them with their rifles. It was a decided check.

The colonel came up.

'We must get on,' he said, but how to do so without useless casualties was not clear. Eventually some petrol was found, but before the Commandos could set fire to the building Lieutenant O'Flaherty and Trooper Sherington made another desperate attempt to storm it. This time both were badly hit, but recovering themselves with admirable fortitude, succeeded in staggering from the warehouse. Soon afterwards 6 Troop set it on fire, and leaving Lance-Corporal Fyson and another man to watch it, pushed on. When it got stuffy these resolute Germans came out, and walked into a burst of Bren gun fire. They had disdained their chance to surrender.

By this time Captain Hooper with the floating reserve had come ashore and reinforced the attack.

At about this time, 1159 hours to be precise, thirteen Blenheim bombers put in an attack on Herdla aerodrome with 250 pound bombs. One bomber was hit by an 88mm shell and colliding with another, crashed with it into the sea. With more than twenty craters in the runway Herdla was out of action not only for the 27th but for several days to come. Planes from Stavanger and Herdla could no longer

intervene in the fighting at Vaagso

While the Commandos were fighting ashore the destroyers were dealing with the shipping in the fjord.

The *Fohn*, 250 tons, had been detailed to escort a convoy consisting of three ships, which were getting up steam as dawn broke. The *Fohn*, twin Oerlikons, it will be remembered hit a Hampden with disastrous results to 4 Troop, and was herself pierced by two shells, fired solid, by 6 Troop With the *Norma* (2,200 tons) and the *Reimer Etzard Fritzen* (3,000 tons) she fled northwards but the flat-bottomed schuyt *Eismeer* (1,000 tons) had not got up steam. She hoisted the Dutch flag but this ruse did not save her for long Exchanging fire in an unequal fight with *Onslow* and *Oribi* the German flotilla made off, while Leutnant zur See Lohr tried to get rid of *Fohn*, confidential code books. He was killed by a shell from *Onslow* just as he was about to drop them overboard. All three vessels ran themselves aground and the crew of *Fohn*, armed with rifles, engaged the destroyers from the rocky shore until *Onslow's* gunfire drove them off. Lieutenant-Commander de Costabadie, DSC, veteran of Dunkirk and one of Mountbatten's Planning Staff, boarded *Fohn* and after an exchange of rifle fire with her crew carried off her code books, the major intelligence scoop of the Vaagso raid. They gave the radio call sign of every German vessel in Norway and France besides details of their challenges, countersigns and emergency signals. Moreover, the Germans had no reason to suppose that Lohr had not dropped them, bound in lead into the icy depths of Ulvesund.

The *Eismeer* seemed ripe for capture, but, as de Costabadie approached her in a whaler, the seaman pulling the stroke oar was mortally wounded by a bullet from the town. The party got aboard but were prevented by rifle fire from raising the anchor. Captain Armstrong *(Onslow)*, compelled to admit a stalemate, called back his landing party and sank *Eismeer* by gunfire. Soon after, much to her own crew's surprise, *Onslow* managed to dispose of a German aircraft with an antique 4-inch gun which she had recently had mounted aft. On the 28th Armstrong wrote in his report:

Yesterday was excellent for a new ship. At one moment we were sinking merchant vessel with the after 4.7, covering the military with the foremost 4.7, engaging aircraft with a inch, and the close range weapons were covering the landing party against German snipers. Unfortunately there was no torpedo target.'

At 1000 hours *Oribi* had landed Group 5, Captain Birney's half troop from 2 Commando, which had set up an ambush at the hamlet of Rodberg in order to prevent German reinforcements coming south from Halsor. This done, *Oribi* had moved to assist *Onslow*, and had helped her dispose of the armed tug *Rechtenfleth* (200 tons) and the *Anita L M Russ* (2,800 tons) which came sailing innocently down Ulvesund and made the – literally – fatal error of mistaking the British for German destroyers.

The Halsor battery had been attacked by three Blenheims early in the day, but little damage had been done. The commander, Leutnant

Lienkamp, heard heavy firing from South Vaagso, but could not get through on the telephone, perhaps because Sebelin had thrown the telephone orderlies into the fight. The Headquarters of the 181st Division, to which the garrison belonged, did not really know what was going on, though observers on Rugsundo had seen warships and landing craft approach Maaloy. Lienkamp, told rather vaguely to find out what was happening sent out his infantry platoon as a fighting patrol. They had a shooting match with Birney, and lost two men.

The Commandos blew the road before re-embarking, covered by a heavy fire from *Onslow* and *Oribi*. They had no casualties.

In the town the arrival of Hooper's troop had given a new impetus to the attack. Lieutenant G D Black and his section pushed forward to the left of the main road, carrying with it men of 1 and 3 Troops, and driving the Germans before them. Black himself was hit in the forearm by a fleeing German, who swung round and fired a burst with his Schmeisser machine pistol. Asked later what he thought

The destruction of a warehouse on the waterfront

Above: Sergeant Chitty shepherds prisoners. *Below:* Norwegian refugees embar[k]
Right: Second-Lieutenant O'Flaherty is wounded

of the Schmeisser as a weapon, Black, a Canadian, commented cooly: 'Well, I reckon a two-inch group at a hundred yards isn't too bad.'

Along the main street Colonel Durnford-Slater, with his runners, was still advancing. He came up with 6 Troop as they broke into a large house. There was a motor car outside from which it seemed possible that it was the German commander's billet. For once there was no resistance. A careful research revealed only one German, who lay trembling in bed in an upstairs room. 'Let him be,' said Durnford-Slater. This was undoubtedly Major Schroeder, who had been mortally wounded by a shell-burst at the beginning of the fight and carried off to his quarters. There was suspicious movement in a neighbouring building and some of 6 Troop opened fire from an upper window of Schroeder's billet. It seems not unlikely that the men who brought him there to die had slipped out as 6 Troop broke in the front door.

By this time the 6 Troop party had dwindled to half its original strength, casualties, escorts and messengers having diminished it. Worst of all the commander of another troop had taken it upon himself to order Sergeant Connolly's sub-section to carry some of the dead and wounded back to the beach. Durnford-Slater, however, had collected some of 2 Troop and these with his runners were about equal in numbers to the 6 Troop party, which now advanced and took cover along the bank of a small stream. The colonel led his party forward covered by them, and it was now that a curious episode occurred. A German sailor emerged from a side lane, flung a stick grenade at the colonel, and promptly put his hands up. Durnford-Slater dived into a doorway escaping with minor injuries, but both the orderlies who flanked him were badly hurt.

Sergeant Mills, rifle at the hip, advanced towards the German with purposeful mien.

'Nein, nein' cried the sailor.

'Ja, ja!' said Mills, and shot him.

'Yeah, well, Mills, you shouldn't have done that,' was all the colonel said.

This was practically the end of the fighting. About 1145 hours the colone held a brief conference in a garden ordered Captain Bradley (1 Troop) to destroy the Firda Factory and pu 6 Troop into a good solid house to ac as a 'stop' in case the Germans shoul counterattack before the demolition were complete. At 1300 hours, b which time all firing had long sinc ceased, this party withdrew.

The re-embarkation went withou hitch, demolitions continuing almos to the last moment. By 1445 hours the troops were back aboard.

Kenya took a hit from the Rugsund battery at about midday and *Princ Charles* sustained some damage fron a bombing attack as the expeditio was putting to sea. *Oribi* had a fev minor casualties, and the land forc lost twenty killed (of whom six, in cluding Captain Giles, were buried a sea), and fifty-seven wounded. Severa aircraft were lost. Not a single British prisoner was taken.

The departing raiders left a fair trai of destruction behind them. Every man of the Maaloy battery was killed or taken, its guns were destroyed, it barracks ruined. A number of fac tories, including the Firda Factory were burnt or blown up. So were the telephone exchanges, the Seternes lighthouse, and a number of ware houses. The Germans' only tank, a French one, had been blown up in its garage.

At about 1230 hours *Offa* and *Chid dingfold* had disposed of the armed trawler *Donner* (250 tons) and the *Anhalt* (5,930 tons) off the mouth of the fjord, bringing the total of shipping sunk to 15,630 tons.

On 28th December General Kurt Woytasch, the commander of 181 Divi sion, arrived in South Vaagso to sur vey the damage. It is not easy to be sure exactly how many men the Germans had lost, for no figures seem to be available for a detachment of twenty-five men, who were in the town for the Christmas holiday. The infantry garrison lost eleven killed, seven wounded, and sixteen missing— mostly captured. The marine detach ment lost six. The Halsor platoon had two casualties, and the Rugsund battery, which had made a consider able nuisance of itself with an old Russian 130mm gun (its other was non-

Above: A group of officers pose on the return voyage. Second from the right, behind the capstan, is Captain Ronald. *Right:* Mr John Nygaardsvold, Norwegian Prime Minister in exile

operational), had lost only one killed and eight wounded. Every man of the Maaloy battery was killed or captured. In all the German casualties must have been somewhere between 110 and 130, excluding those sustained by the crews of the eight ships sunk. One Norwegian civilian was killed and five slightly wounded. The damage to Norwegian property exceeded 5,000,000 Kroner.

Though some seventy volunteers returned to the United Kingdom the Norwegian Government in exile was not at all pleased with the results of the raid. The aged Prime Minister, Mr. Nygaardsvold, expressed his opinion very forcibly:

Who could be so blind as to delude himself that this effort could have done anything to shorten the ordeal of Norway? Undoubtedly the enemy had been annoyed by the very impudence of the operation lancing deep into the shoreline he sought to secure, but it could have only one result: the Germans would now strengthen their defences, making the ultimate victory even harder to achieve than it would have been if the raid had never taken place'.

In one respect he was quite right. The Germans certainly did build up their defences. But since the Allies had no intention of invading Norway that could only do good.

If Nygaardsvold was ruffled, Hitler was infuriated by the Vaagso raid. Even before the blow fell OKW, the German Headquarters in Berlin, had been concerned about possible operations in Scandinavia now that America was in the war on the Allied side. On Christmas Day a fresh appreciation of the situation in Norway had been ordered.

General von Falkenhorst had taken advantage of this to ask for 12,000 replacements in order to bring his divisions up to strength, and three additional divisions to increase his reserves and give more depth to his defensive layout.

On top of Falkenhorst's report came news of Operations 'Archery' and 'Anklet', their effect reinforced by the mining of the troopship *Kong Ring*, with men going on leave, in the North Sea.

Hitler lost no time in demanding of his military advisers their interpretation of these sinister events. Were the British contemplating a larger landing in Norway in order to menace the German coastal shipping? Before the end of the year Hitler had delivered his own verdict:

'If the British go about things properly, they will attack northern Norway at several points. By means of an all-out attack by their fleet and ground troops they will try to displace us there, take Narvik if possible, and thus exert pressure on Sweden and Finland. This might be of decisive importance for the outcome of the war.

'The German fleet must therefore use all its forces for the defence of Norway. It would be expedient to transfer all battleships and pocket battleships there for this purpose.'

With *Scharnhorst* and *Gneisenau* bottled up in Brest the admirals hoped the Führer would change his mind but in mid-January he sent for Grand Admiral Raeder and told him: 'Norway is the zone of destiny in this war. I demand unconditional obedience to my commands and directives concerning the defence of this area.'

Meanwhile a cornucopia was pouring gifts upon Falkenhorst. First his 12,000 replacements arrived, then came 18,000 men organized as fortress battalions. An armoured division was activated in Norway to act as a mobile reserve. Good new German coast defence guns were provided to replace antiques like the Russian and Belgian

Top left: Colonel-General von Falkenhorst. *Top right:* Field-Marshal List during his visit of inspection to Norway, on the deck of a U-Boat in Oslo harbour. *Right:* Germans patrol the shores of a Norwegian fjord

guns which had defended Vaagsfjord on 27th December.

In February 1942 Generalfeldmarshall List, as the Führer's personal representative, made a tour of inspection and on his recommendation three more divisional commands were established in Norway, more coast artillery was sent there, and defensive positions were built up in the interior. The process continued until, on 6th June 1944, the day when the Allies landed in Normandy, the German garrison in Norway was 372,000 strong. One wonders what difference even 100,000 of these might have made to the fighting in France or White Russia. The Germans in Normandy were decidedly short of good infantry.

The battleship *Tirpitz* sailed from the Baltic and reached Norway in safety. Then on 11th February 1942 *Scharnhorst*, *Gneisenau* and *Prinz Eugen* broke out of Brest and, taking advantage of foul weather, made their desperate dash up the English Channel. In the Straits of Dover *Gneisenau* was so hard hit that she had to put into Kiel, where British bombers holed her again before the month was out. *Scharnhorst*, too, was hit but got through to Norway, where, eventually, she was joined by *Gneisenau*. *Prinz Eugen* reached Trondheim, but a torpedo had taken off her rudder and she was compelled to return to Germany for repairs.

Great was the indignation of the British public when these three ships escaped up Channel, but their concentration in Norwegian waters greatly lightened the Admiralty's task, simply because they were so much easier to watch and to keep out of the North Atlantic. In March and April *Hipper* and *Lützow* joined them.

In the Vaagso raid the British hazarded a small flotilla, the equivalent of a weak battalion and half a dozen squadrons of aircraft. Seldom in the history of warfare have such rewards been gained for so small a stake. *Archery* was the code name of the Vaagso raid. It was not inappropriate: the arrow struck the gold.

Scharnhorst and Gneisenau dash up the Channel. Picture taken from the Prinz Engen

St Nazaire

'Anyone who even thinks of doing such a thing deserves the DSO.' A Planner at Combined Operations HQ. 'This is not an ordinary raid, it is an operation of war.' Lord Louis Mountbatten 13th March 1942

St Nazaire has been called the greatest raid of all. It was certainly the most desperate. Its main object was to destroy the great gates of the only dry dock, the Forme Ecluse, on the Atlantic coast of France, which was capable of taking the German battleship *Tirpitz*. A secondary, but still important, aim was to do as much damage as possible to the U-boat bunkers and the docks.

The *Bismarck*, the sister ship of the *Tirpitz*, had been sunk on 27th May 1941 whilst making for St Nazaire. In early 1942 the *Tirpitz* herself was actually in Norwegian waters, but it was suspected from intelligence received that she was preparing for a foray into the Atlantic. The Admiralty, ignorant of the Führer's reactions to the Vaagso raid, was not to know that the Germans were far from contemplating a cruise that would bring the *Tirpitz* anywhere near St Nazaire.

The planning of the operation presented peculiar difficulties. Not only was the target 250 miles from Falmouth, the nearest British port; it was six miles up the River Loire Moreover there were no beaches.

The military force selected for the raid consisted of Number 2 Commando (Lieutenant-Colonel A C Newman) and demolition parties, eighty strong in all, drawn from Numbers 1, 3, 4, 5, 9 and 12 Commandos. They were trained and led by Captain W H Pritchard, RE

Planning began in February and there was time for a certain amount of training, which was conducted in conditions of great secrecy. The demolition parties were assembled as though for a course of instruction and, when they had received their specialist training, were concentrated aboard the landing ship *Princess Josephine Charlotte* at Falmouth.

Number 2 Commando, whose cadre had come from the Independent Companies, had now been in existence for nearly two years, and had been thoroughly well trained in night movement, the techniques of sur-

Lieutenant-Colonel Charles Newman VC

mounting all kinds of obstacles at speed, route finding, night firing and all the other skills so vital to the raider. Its commander was a rugged territorial infantry officer, with an original turn of mind. As a climax to its training the force was sent on a trip round the Scilly Isles in motor launches in weather so rough that the hardiest were seasick.

A final examination of air photographs showed four newly installed coast defence gun positions in the middle of the dock area. To deal with these thirty Commando soldiers were added to the force, bringing the total to 265 all ranks. Newman paid a visit to Combined Operations Headquarters in Richmond Terrace on 13th March, and after a final briefing session with Mountbatten and his staff left for Falmouth in a staff car. He reached Tavistock that night and 'spent an uneasy night locked in his hotel bedroom with all the plans'. He had left London in somewhat sombre mood— as well he might—but arriving at Falmouth he found his followers in high spirits, their training nearly completed.

There was still time for a full dress rehearsal, an exercise 'to test the defences' of Devonport dockyard. In this the whole force, except the destroyer *Campbelltown*, took part, while the defenders were reinforced by the local Home Guard. Practically everything went wrong, and the defenders were jubilant.

Meanwhile the cover plan was being developed. The force was called the 10th Anti-Submarine Striking Force, and it was discreetly made known that it was to carry out long-range anti-submarine sweeps, far beyond the Western Approaches. It was rumoured that the force was going overseas, and tropical kit, naval sun helmets and so forth were to be seen being smuggled aboard. How much of all this got back to the Germans cannot be told. The funnels of the destroyer *Campbelltown*, which had a vital part to play, were cut down to make her resemble a German *Möwe* class torpedo boat. The last air photographs received before the expedition set sail showed four torpedo boats of that class, berthed alongside the very spot in the dockyard which Newman had selected

for his Command Post. Commander R E D Ryder, the naval force commander, suggested that Newman's reserve, which was only twelve strong, would be needed to deal with them. Newman was unmoved by this dismal intelligence.

The force left Falmouth on the afternoon of 26th March, sailing at fourteen knots in three columns. The midships column consisted of the Hunt class destroyers HMS *Atherstone* and *Tynedale*, the old American destroyer *Buchanan*, which had been renamed *Campbelltown*, and Motor Gun Boat (MGB) 314. The port and starboard columns were made up of motor launches (MLs). At first the weather was rather rough for the MLs, but the wind fell gradually and the night was calm, hazy and moonlit.

There were only two incidents during the voyage. On the second day out a German U-boat was seen on the surface. *Tynedale* opened fire and depth charges were dropped. The expedition was steering a course for La Pallice but even so Ryder had to make up his mind whether the submarine had signalled the presence of the force. Should he turn back? He did no such thing, and, as is now known, the U-boat had in fact reported only the presence of the destroyers. Presumably the MLs were too low in the water for her lookout to spot. Later some French trawlers were encountered. One, *Le Slack*, was boarded, and though nothing suspicious was discovered, her crew were put aboard the *Atherstone*.

Night fell and at 2000 hours the force hove to, as yet undiscovered, for the HQ staff to transfer to MGB 314. At 2200 hours a light from HM Submarine *Sturgeon*, the navigational beacon, was seen right ahead, and the force, flying German colours, began the run in. MGB 314 was leading, with *Campbelltown* (Lieutenant-Commander S H Beattie) next, then fourteen MLs in two columns, with Motor Torpedo Boat 74 bringing up the rear. Meanwhile bombers of the RAF were attacking St Nazaire through low cloud and the trails of German tracer could be seen mounting skywards.

The expedition had safely negotiated the dangerous mud flats when at 0122 hours searchlights were suddenly

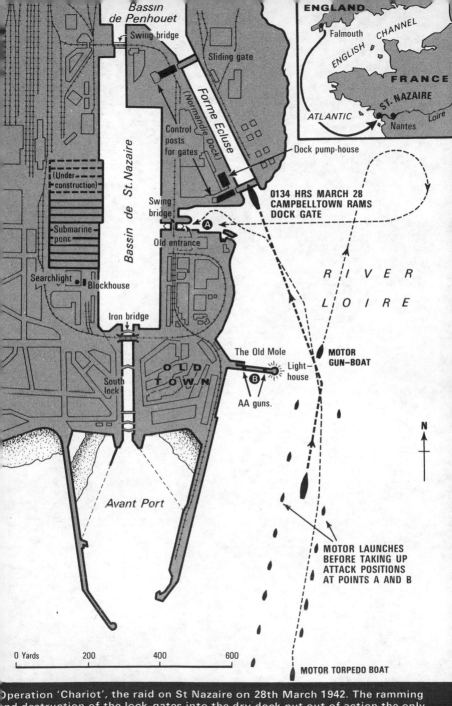

ENGLAND

ENGLISH CHANNEL

Falmouth

FRANCE

ATLANTIC

ST. NAZAIRE

Nantes

Loire

Bassin de Penhouet

Swing bridge

Sliding gate

Forme Ecluse (Normandie Dock)

Control posts for gates

Dock pump-house

(Under construction)

Submarine pens

Bassin de St. Nazaire

Swing bridge

Old entrance

A

0134 HRS MARCH 28
CAMPBELLTOWN RAMS
DOCK GATE

Searchlight

Blockhouse

Iron bridge

South lock

R I V E R

L O I R E

The Old Mole

Light-house

B

AA guns.

O L D
T O W N

MOTOR
GUN-BOAT

N

Avant Port

MOTOR LAUNCHES
BEFORE TAKING UP
ATTACK POSITIONS
AT POINTS A AND B

0 Yards   200   400   600

MOTOR TORPEDO BOAT

Operation 'Chariot', the raid on St Nazaire on 28th March 1942. The ramming
and destruction of the lock-gates into the dry dock put out of action the only
dry dock outside German waters capable of accommodating the mighty *Tirpitz*.

Left: Commander RED Ryder VC. *Above:* Lieutenant-Commander R H Beattie VC

switched on from both banks and the force was challenged. Leading Signalman Pike, disguised as a German petty officer, signalled back giving the call sign of a German torpedo boat, learned from *Föhn's* code book taken at Vaagso. He required the shore batteries to wait, adding in plain language, that two craft, damaged by enemy action, requested permission to proceed to harbour without delay. On this the few guns which had already opened up ceased fire, though those on the north bank were not long silent. MGB 314 then made the international signal for ships being fired on by friendly forces.

These ruses, all perfectly legitimate, won the force a good five minutes, and when at 0127 hours the Germans opened up in earnest *Campbelltown* was already past the heaviest batteries. Hauling down her German colours, she ran up the White Ensign and opened fire. Tracer began to fly in all directions, and a German guard ship, hit time and again by both sides, was sunk. The fire of the British flotilla was extremely effective and after three or four minutes the German fire began to slacken. 'A triumph', as Ryder said, 'for the many gunlayers in the coastal craft and in the *Campbelltown.*'

Nothing could stop the old destroyer now, and at 0134 hours, four minutes late, she crashed into the lock gates at nineteen knots. There was a staggering shock as her bows cleaved into the great caissons. The main object of the raid had been achieved before a single Commando soldier had set foot ashore.

Now began a fight of almost incredible complexity, as assault and demolition parties rushed to carry out their varied tasks. In general, Newman's plan was to form a bridgehead and to cut off the approaches to the dockyard area from the rest of the town.

A party under RSM Moss had been detailed to seize Newman's selected Command Post, but the motor launch this group was in was sunk. The RSM struck out for the shore, towing some of his men on a Carly float, but this gallant effort ended when a searchlight came on and the whole group was wiped out by machine-gun fire.

When the colonel and the eight men of his party landed from the MGB they were, of course, unaware of what had befallen the RSM's party and 'flying timber, smoke, sparks, and flames made it impossible to see very clearly'. Making for his Command Post Newman 'literally bumped into a German' who promptly surrendered. From him the colonel made out that the building he had selected as his HQ was in fact a German one. He sent his prisoner to tell his comrades to surrender, but at this instant a gun opened up at point-blank range, compelling the commandos to take cover. Two vessels from the inner basin and two guns from the roof of the U-boat bunker and a battery on the south bank of the river joined in, and soon the small HQ party was under very heavy fire Troop Sergeant-Major Haines came up with part of Captain Hooper's special task force, whose main task was to destroy two guns between the Old Mole and the Old Entrance. He opened fire with a 2-inch mortar and managed to silence the guns on the U-boat bunker for a time.

One of the demolition parties under Second-Lieutenant H Pennington (Number 4 Commando) never got ashore, but the others lost no time in getting on with their many tasks. Lieutenant Stuart Chant (5 Commando), was hit by shrapnel in the right arm and left leg whilst still aboard the *Campbelltown*. He estimated that something like seventy-five per cent of those on her deck were hit before she rammed the lock gates. He and his men climbed from her bows down scaling ladders and ran like hell to the pumping station. Captain D Roy's assault party had made short work of the gunners on the roof. Chant's men blew the lock off the steel door and went down the steel staircase to lay their charges forty feet below ground. Later Chant described this episode:

'My hands had been cut with small pieces of shell which made the handling of the charge somewhat awkward but Sergeant Dockerill stayed with me in case my wounds should prevent me from firing the charges, while I sent the rest of the party upstairs to warn

Lieutenant Stuart Chant

the neighbourhood of the coming explosion.

'We raced outside and lay on the ground completely exposed on the concrete paving. Fortunately we shifted a further ten yards away a second later, for when the explosion did come huge concrete blocks hurtled through the air perilously near.

'After the explosion we took our remaining explosives in our rucksacks and raced back to the pumping station to complete the work of destruction by blowing up the electric motors and installations'.

They found that the motors had been pitched down below by the collapse of the floor: 'So we just did a little quiet wrecking with sledge hammers and incendiaries'.

Meanwhile Lieutenant Smalley and his party had completely destroyed the winding station near by. These bangs were music in the colonel's ears and he and his HQ party now took up their prearranged position to cover the demolition parties as they fell back across the bridge towards the Old Mole. By this time demolitions were going on all over the place. Newman was joined by his second-in-command, Major Copland, who had landed from the *Campbelltown*. He reported that of one assault party, only the commander, Captain M C Burn, had managed to swim ashore from a stricken ML. He was saved from drowning by Corporal Arthur Young, who grabbed his hair and dragged him along until he reached the Mole. Newman now decided to withdraw Captain Roy's party which was forming a bridgehead on the north side of the connection between the Old Entrance and the Bassin de St Nazaire. Despite the very heavy fire Lance-Corporal Harrington, as cool as if he was on a training exercise at home, got through to Captain Roy with the colonel's message.

Chant, withdrawing his party towards the Old Mole, came to the iron bridge which was covered by a gun in an adjoining building.

'I therefore ordered the men to swing hand by hand, monkey fashion, along the girders under the bridge. Thus we all got across safely unobserved'.

'We gained some railway lines

among the warehouses and joined more returning parties. Then came the blow: Colonel Newman told us: "This is where we walk home. All the boats have been blown up or have gone back." '

Newman now had about seventy officers and men with him, but more than half had been hit. The men were behaving magnificently and there was no question of surrender. He held a brief conference with his surviving officers. Some suggested manning some tugs and trying to escape down river.

'Another plan,' wrote Chant, 'was to go down the quayside and swim or wade upstream until we were clear of the German defenders. Colonel Newman, however, decided that the best route was to fight our way back through the warehouses to the east until we reached the bridge.'

The colonel's idea was that the survivors should break up into small groups and make for the Spanish frontier. He ordered them not to surrender until all their ammunition had been used up, and not to surrender at all if they could help it. Their best chance, he said, was to find their way through the town into the open country. 'It's a lovely moonlight night for it.'

Led by Captain Roy and an assault party they moved off and reached the south bank of the Bassin de St Nazaire opposite the U-boat pens. Here Chant was hit in the right knee by a ricochet. His men carried him a little way, but he ordered them to leave him.

'I watched the remainder of the party go south, towards the old part of the town, and then bear right and dash across the swing bridge into the main town. It was bright moonlight, and I could see them clearly. They were fired on from pillboxes and buildings near the bridge; I could see other troops, believed to be Germans, climbing about on the roofs of those buildings.'

The main body, a dwindling band, pushed on, jumping over walls, traversing back gardens, and bursting through houses back to the road.

A German armoured car dashed past 'spitting fire from the turret on all and sundry, including Germans'. Newman's men dodged up an alley. The ituation became more and more confused. A German motor-cycle and sidecar was shot up, and the rider and passenger killed.

Eventually Newman, with the twenty or so men who were still with him, took cover in a 'very convenient air raid cellar, complete with mattresses'. Here he intended to stay until next night, when the men would make for the open country in pairs.

'I also decided that if we were found in the cellar I would surrender, as the wounded were in a pretty bad way, and a single hand grenade flung down the stairs would see the lot off.'

Here, some time later, a German party came upon them and accepted Newman's surrender. His men were taken to German headquarters and taken in lorries to a café at La Boule where prisoners were being collected.

Chant, who had been joined by a soldier from another party, was found by three SS men with machine-pistols. 'Heraus! Heraus!' they shouted. 'The soldier with me then stood up with his hands up. He was shot dead from a range of one yard by all three men.' They saw that Chant was wounded and carried him into a café where there were other wounded Commando soldiers.

The brunt of the fighting had fallen on the parties landed from the *Campbelltown* for the MLs had had a very rough time on the run in. Those of the port column were meant to land their troops on the Old Mole. Only one was not destroyed or disabled and only a handful of the men got ashore. Lieutenant I B Henderson, RNVR, unable to bring ML 306 alongside the Old Mole made for the Old Entrance, and, failing to land the Commandos there, turned for home. Some miles downstream he fought an unequal duel with a German MTB. Sergeant Durrant, manning a twin Lewis gun, though riddled with bullets maintained his fire until he collapsed 'sagging over his gun' and died of wounds. With its captain killed and every man aboard dead or wounded the ML was compelled to surrender.

Of the starboard column only the sixth, ML 177, got its party ashore

After the raid, prisoners are rounded up in a bar

The Sten Gun Mk II
The name is derived from the first
letters of the inventors' names
(Sheppard and Tarpin) and the first
letters of Enfield, where the gun was
developed. A cheap and easily produced
weapon, it was made in millions and
was a valued tool of resistance forces
all over Europe. In experienced hands it
was surprisingly accurate and – legend
notwithstanding – perfectly safe for
the user.

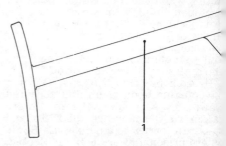

1. Steel tube butt
2. Backsight
3. Block return spring
4. Trigger pin
5. Trigger

Rate of fire: 500/550 rounds
per minute *Magazine capacity:* 32
rounds, 9mm *Effective range:* 80 yards
Weight: 6.62 lbs *Length:* 30 inches
Muzzle velocity: 1,280 feet per second.

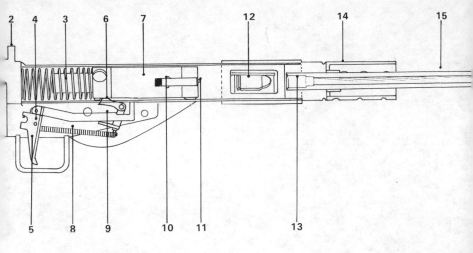

6. Sear
7. Breech block assembly
8. Trigger return spring
9. Trip lever
10. Extractor

11. Firing pin
12. 32 9mm rounds
13. Chamber
14. Barrel sleeve
15. Barrel

HMS Campbelltown wedged in to the
sluice gate

more or less intact. TSM Haines landed at the Old Entrance and 'did valiant work all through the operation'. A number of other soldiers managed to swim ashore from abandoned craft, but without weapons.

Three MLs (156, 270 and 446) and the MGB, her decks slippery with blood, reached the rendezvous with *Atherstone* some miles off the estuary of the Loire.

Immediately after the Campbelltown blew up

Meanwhile *Tynedale* had fought an inconclusive action with five German MTBs, and had been hit twice. The crew of ML 156 and the wounded from MGB 314 were transferred to the *Atherstone*, while those from MLs 270 and 446 were put aboard *Tynedale*. The two destroyers, escorted by aircraft of Coastal Command, got back to Falmouth safely. MLs 160, 307 and 443, under Lieutenant T D L Platt, RNR, managed to struggle home on their own. They had hardly a gallon of fuel left. Astonishing though it may seem

they had shot down a German aircraft and damaged another.

When dawn broke after that wild night in St Nazaire there was the old *Campbelltown* 'stuck fast in the lock gates'. Gradually German officers assembled to inspect this phenomenon, while other ranks looked on from the dockside and speculated as to why the British should have carried out such an extraordinary operation. About noon, when there were some forty officers aboard and perhaps 400 German onlookers ashore, the five tons of explosives in the bows of the *Campbelltown* blew up.

There were further explosions at 1630 and 1730 hours when delayed action torpedoes fired through the Old Entrance by MTB 74 went up in the Bassin de St Nazaire. Scenes of considerable confusion ensued, with panicky German soldiers shooting French dock workers, as many as 300 of whom are said to have died, and even members of their own Todt organization. It is said that the panic spread as far inland as Nantes, where

After the raid, an aerial view shows the Campbelltown without her bows 500 yards inside the lock

The aftermath. *Top left:* German troops pass a dead British sergeant *Bottom left:* Soldiers and sailors being led away. *Above:* British pass the bier of a dead comrade

the wives and mistresses of German officers were reported, somewhat improbably, to have run wildly into the streets screaming that the invasion of Europe had begun.

In this raid the Royal Navy lost thirty-one officers and 751 ratings; the Commandos thirty-four officers and 178 other ranks. Five of those left behind managed to make their way back to England via Spain. They were Corporal Wheeler; Lance-Corporals Douglas, Howarth and Sims, and Private Harding. Their success says much for the tenacity and initiative bred by Commando training.

Five Victoria Crosses were awarded for this desperate action. They went to Commander Ryder, Lieutenant-Commander S H Beattie of the *Campbelltown*, to Lieutenant-Colonel Charles Newman, whose resolute spirit had carried his unit to such heights of daring and devotion, and posthumously to Able Seaman Savage and Sergeant Durrant.

The battleship *Tirpitz*, whose potential menace had led to the launching of the raid, remained in the fjords of Norway until in September 1944 12,000 pound bombs from Lancasters of the RAF capsized her near Tromsö.

At the funeral, German officers salute captured British officers

Alarums and excursions

'There comes from the sea a hand of steel which plucks the German sentries from their posts.'
Winston S Churchill 1942.

The exponents of the *Blitzkrieg*, so successful in the period 1939-1941, stirred up a bitter resentment which led their victims to fight back by all means in their power. In every occupied country resistance movements grew up, their morale raised by the numerous exploits of British and Allied Commandos, which were faithfully passed on to them by the British Broadcasting Corporation. A time came when no German officer could lie easy in his bed whether in Narvik, Athens or Bayonne. Only at home in the Reich could the dashing Teuton sleep secure, and there his slumbers would be disturbed by the RAF.

As the war went on the landing operations planned by Combined Operations Headquarters became ever larger and more ambitious, Lofoten,

Vaagso, St Nazaire and Dieppe were all relatively large-scale affairs compared to the raids laid on by Dudley Clarke in 1940. Yet the pin-prick raids carried out by a handful of enterprising and gallant officers and men deserve their place in these pages, if only because they contributed to the general sense of unease which gradually came to pervade the German garrisons of northwest Europe.

But before turning to the smaller raids of 1942 some mention of the Commando system of training seems timely, for it was at this period that an organization tailored for the special requirements of the Commandos came into being.

In December 1942 Achnacarry Castle, the seat of Sir Donald Cameron of Lochiel, the chief of Clan Cameron, became the Commando Depot. For the remainder of the war it was commanded with marked success by Lieutenant-Colonel Charles Vaughan, who had previously been second-in-command of Number 4 Commando. Vaughan had had twenty-eight years service in the Coldstream Guards and the Buffs and knew a very great deal

At Athnacarry, Lieutenant-Colonel Charles Vaughan casts a critical eye over Free French Commandos

Training in Scotland. Commandos practice clearing a landing craft

At Inverary, Major Jack Churchill, sword in hand, leads men of 3 Commando ashore from a Eureka

Left and above: Training for the cliff assault. *Below:* In the mountains of Scotland, Commandos learn the techniques of survival

about the ways of the Army. He knew exactly what he wanted and he knew how to get it. His rugged determination to exact the last ounce from his trainees was relieved by a warm heart and a bluff sense of humour, and, though possessed of all the dignity of a former Regimental-Sergeant-Major, he could see a joke against himself. Many were the names in which he rejoiced, ranging from Lord Fort William to The Wolf of Badenoch and The Rommel of the North, but the one which seemed somehow to suit him best was The Laird of Achnacarry. Certainly he loved the place and was fiercely determined that the men who survived his course there and passed out to wear the green beret should do it credit. First and last it is thought that as many as 25,000 men, including US Rangers, Belgians, Dutchmen, Frenchmen, Norwegians and Poles passed through his hands. Vaughan had a hand-picked staff, skilled in devising and running realistic exercises of every kind. Live ammunition was used as a matter of course, and it says much for the skill of the instructors that no more than about forty fatal casualties were suffered during the three years in which the depot was in existence. Feats of activity, such as the celebrated Death Ride in which men crossed the River Arkaig by sliding down a rope, caught the imagination of countless trainees. Men like Alick Cowieson, alias Alick Mor, of the Cameron Highlanders, and CQMS Frickleton, the chief PT instructor, and deviser of the Tarzan Course, displayed a fiendish ingenuity in thinking out such entertainments.

Life at Achnacarry was rugged from the moment the trainees reached Spean Bridge railway station. If they expected transport to take them to the depot they were disappointed: they marched. It is on record that on one occasion an American Ranger, newly arrived, addressed an instructor, Sergeant Taffy Edwards:

'Hey sarge, where's the nearest bar?'
'It's down that way.'
'Yeah? Is it far?'
'No, not far. Only seven miles. It's at Spean Bridge – where your train arrived.'

It does not rain all the time at Achnacarry, but it would be hard to persuade the men who passed through the Commando Depot that that is the case. Far away from the bright lights the men ran up and down mountains by day, became physically fit and acquired confidence and skill at arms. In the evenings, for the good of their souls and in the interests of discipline, they cleaned their brasses, until the day came when their particular intake passed out and Charles Vaughan gave them his closing address:

'When you leave here you will go to civvy billets and get a special allowance. Don't imagine you get this for nothing. You will go on raids and operations.

'Some of you will be wounded. Perhaps badly. Maybe you will lose a leg, or an arm. I tell you now, you don't have to worry. You will be taken care of.' (Dramatic pause) 'There will always be a job for you – up here at Achnacarry.'

To return to the operations, on the night 11th/12th April 1942, Captain Gerald Montanaro RE, accompanied by Trooper Preece, canoed into Boulogne harbour, stuck a limpet (magnetic) mine on a German tanker and withdrew unseen. His canoe was leaky and he was picked up by his parent craft, ML 102, when he was practically waterlogged. Air photographs taken next day showed that the tanker was even more waterlogged – and minus her funnel. Montanaro was awarded the DSO.

The smallest yet one of the best Commando organizations was the Special-Scale Raiding Force, formed by Major Gus March-Phillips, DSO, MBE, Captain J G Appleyard, MC, and Graham Hayes, MC. With the welcoming cooperation of its owner, Mr Stevenson, they formed a base at Anderson Manor, a charming Elizabethan house not far from Poole Harbour, and set out to plague the enemy.

Their first expedition (14th/15th August 1942) was an attempt to destroy an anti-aircraft gun near Cape Barfleur. They launched a Goatley collapsible boat from an MTB, but, landing in the wrong place, failed to find their objective. They did, however, kill three Germans.

On the night 2nd/3rd September Appleyard carried out a skilful raid

Captain Gerald Montanaro

on the Casquet Lighthouse, which the Germans, since they took the Channel Islands in 1940, had been using as a naval signalling station. In a letter Appleyard described the midnight adventure:

'I navigated again for the whole job. It was pretty nerve-racking as it's a notoriously evil place and you get a tremendous tide race round the rocks. However, all went well, and we found the place all right, and pushed in our landing craft. My job in the landing and embarkation was 'bow-man'.

'I was the first to leap for the rock, taking a light line with me, and then had to hold the landing craft up to the rock on the bowline whilst Graham [Hayes], in the stern, held the boat off the rock with a stern-line and kedge-anchor he had dropped on the approach, so as to prevent her being dashed on the rock by the swell. There was quite a hefty swell surging up the rocks, and it felt pretty weird in the dark, but we got the whole party ashore safely. The boat was then hauled off the rock on the stern-line by Graham (who remained in her) and I handed over the bowline to the other man who was staying with the boat, and then she rode quite happily until our return.'

They made their way through the barbed wire and gained the courtyard unchallenged. There they dispersed to their pre-arranged objectives. Appleyard and Sergeant Winter dashed up the spiral staircase to the light room,

to find it empty. The garrison was taken completely by surprise. Three were in bed, two were turning in, and two were doing odd jobs. Not a shot was fired, though the Germans had an Oerlikon and two boxes of grenades open. These were dumped in the sea, and then with nineteen men in their landing craft the raiders set off for home. Appleyard was the only casualty. He broke the tibia of a leg whilst re-embarking. They reached Portsmouth to learn that Cherbourg had been 'frantically calling up the Casquets'.

On the night 7th/8th September Major March-Phillips led his men in a raid on St Honoré near the Cherbourg peninsula. Appleyard, because of his damaged shinbone, acted as Navigating Officer. March-Phillips, Hayes and nine others made up the landing party. Finding the objective more heavily guarded than expected, March-Phillips decided to withdraw and return later with a larger force.

On the way back to the beach, and only about 200 yards from the boat, they ambushed and killed a German patrol of seven men. While the major was searching the bodies for maps and documents, another and stronger patrol was heard approaching, and he swiftly got his party back to their craft. When they had paddled one hundred yards from the shore the Germans illuminated them with a flare and opened a heavy fire, which killed March-Phillips and three men, besides wounding several others, and sank the boat. A voice, thought to be

123

Geoffrey Appleyard

Gus March-Phillips

The pin-prick raids of 1942. Launched by small groups of commandos, these raids were designed merely to harass the German forces in the Channel Islands and on the northern coast of France, with a view to holding German troops in areas where they would not otherwise be needed, and improving the morale of the British and French civilian populations.

Graham Hayes's, was heard calling out that all was lost and urging Appleyard to go away and save his ship. The latter did not, however, depart at once. As he searched for survivors his motor boat was hit and one of her main engines put out of action.

Hayes, who had not been hit and was a very strong swimmer, reached the shore some way from the scene of action, got by 'underground' to Paris and eventually to Spain. The Spaniards handed him over to the Germans, and, after nine months in Fresnes prison, he was shot on 13th July 1943.

A Frenchman, André Desgrange, was also taken. He was kept for a time shackled so that he could only eat from a trough direct by his mouth'. He escaped to Spain, was imprisoned there, and was treated so badly that although phenomenally strong physically he fainted four times under the treatment. He escaped once again, got back to England, and in three to four weeks returned to France as an agent.

Sergeant-Major Tom Winter had swum, unseen, to within about fifty yards of Appleyard's ship when it received a direct hit and moved out to sea. He managed to reach the beach 'where a German attempted to shoot him as he lay gasping for breath at the water's edge'. The man missed. Winter then saw the Germans beat up another of the party who had just struggled ashore, using their stick grenades as clubs. Later this man's life was saved in a German hospital, but after the war he still suffered serious disablement.

Winter for his part was taken to a prison camp in Poland. He found a way of getting in and out by night, and, contacting the Polish underground instead of endeavouring to escape, instructed them in the use of explosives, returning to camp by dawn each morning! The Germans came to suspect him and he was condemned to ten years solitary confinement. The advance of the Russians set him and thousands more prisoners on the march westwards, and eventually he slipped away and reached the Allied lines.

This disaster was not the end of the SBS. As soon as his leg mended Appleyard began raiding again, and on the night 3rd/4th October visited Sark with a hand-picked party of four officers and five men. They learned much of local conditions and something of the defences from an English woman they met, and captured five Germans in the annexe of the Dixcourt Hotel. These men, though captured in bed, recovered sufficiently to attempt to make their escape and four had to be shot. One of these, a powerfully built man, had his hands tied, which was, technically, an infringement of international law, though since he had refused to 'come quiet' it is difficult to blame his captors for securing him. The upshot of this incident was that Commando prisoners taken earlier, at St Nazaire and Dieppe, were handcuffed as a reprisal.

One of the most effective of all the small raids was Operation Musketoon. Captains Gordon Black and Joe Houghton with a detachment of Number 2 Commando and some Norwegians attacked the hydroelectric power station at Glamfjord in Norway. Landing from a French submarine they approached their objective across a black glacier and attacked it about 2300 hours. There was a brief fight in which one of the guards was killed, and then the machinery and a section of the pipeline were destroyed.

Everything had gone according to plan, and the current that supplied the chief aluminium manufacturing plant in Norway had been destroyed. But few of the raiders made their escape. In a clash with a German patrol Black and Houghton were wounded and captured. Taken to Germany, they were shot in consequence of Hitler's notorious 'Commando Order' of 10th October 1942, laying down that his forces should 'slaughter to the last man all those who take part in Commando engagements'.

This order, unlawful by any rules of warfare, is the measure of the effect which an active raiding policy had had on the precarious balance of Hitler's mind.

Dieppe

'Jesus Christ, sir, this is nearly as bad as Achnacarry.'

Dieppe was the biggest raid carried out by the British during the Second World War. Ten major military units took part, only one of which succeeded in taking its objective. Casualties were heavy, and many people found serious fault with the concept of the whole operation. It is as well to recall that it took place approximately halfway between the Dunkirk evacuation, which ended on 4th June 1940, and D-Day, when on 6th June 1944 the Allies invaded Normandy. It was unthinkable that the forces in the United Kingdom should do nothing for four years. The need to show friend and foe alike that Britain was still in the war was in itself sufficient justification for an active raiding policy. Still more important, it was necessary to study the conditions likely to prevail when the Second Front should eventually be launched. There were vital questions to be answered. How strong was Hitler's West Wall? Could the Allies hope to capture a port on D-Day?

There were several reasons for the selection of Dieppe as a target. It was within the range of fighter cover. It was outside any lodgement area likely to be chosen for the D-Day landings. The coast of that part of France has natural defences in its high chalk cliffs, which are similar to those along the English coast between Rottingdean and Newhaven.

The role of capturing Dieppe itself was entrusted to six battalions and an armoured regiment of the 2nd Canadian Infantry Division, which were to land at Puys, Pourville and Dieppe itself. At Berneval and Varengeville were two coast defence batteries, whose guns could bring a crossfire to bear on any ships approaching the beaches. It seemed to the planners that these batteries must be silenced before the main landing. Number 3 Commando was to attack the Berneval Battery and Number 4 that at Varengeville.

Number 4 Commando was commanded by Lieutenant-Colonel the Lord Lovat, MC, whose second-in-command describes him as 'a tall, strikingly handsome fellow who bore

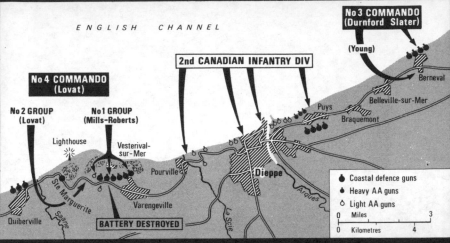

The Raid on Dieppe, 18th/19th August 1942. It was planned to land 6,000 men with full supporting equipment, but the operation proved to be inadequately planned and based on false Intelligence. The verdict: 'a costly but not unfruitful reconnaissance in force'.

Officers of 1st Commando Brigade watch a demonstration of enemy weapons. Lieutenant-Colonel the Lord Lovat sitting on right. Major Derek Mills-Roberts at microphone

himself well and could take life seriously when necessary'.

The idea of raiding Dieppe was first contemplated in April 1942, so there was ample time for planning and training at unit level. Varengeville is three and a half miles west of Dieppe and the battery lay 1,100 yards inland from the cliffs. There were two possible beaches, one at the mouth of the River Saane near Quiberville and the other directly in front of the battery, where there were two gullies, a fault in the cliff. It was decided to use both beaches. The Commando was, therefore, divided into two main groups. Major D Mills-Roberts commanded Number 1 group, with eighty-eight men to provide covering fire, while Lord Lovat commanded 164 men in Number 2 group who were to undertake the assault itself. Lovat's group was the one to land at the mouth of the Saane.

The battery area was reconstructed in outline near Lulworth Cove in Dorset and the Commando rehearsed its full task eight times, until every man could play his part at top speed and carrying his full load of arms,

Dieppe at dawn

mmunition, and whatever else it as his lot to use, be it wireless set, stretcher or demolition charge. Every man was thoroughly briefed with the id of air photographs and a model f the objective. Mills-Roberts wrote: 'The Demolition Party could blow un breeches in their sleep, communications had been tested and counter-tested and the drill for the manning f the assault craft in the Infantry ssault Ship *Prince Albert* had been arried out several times in darkness. 'here was the complete list: it was nteresting to speculate what would o wrong.'

Number 4 Commando had an un-eventful voyage, was roused at about 0100 hours, breakfasted without en-thusiasm, listened to the CO's final pep talk in the wardroom, and filed to boat stations.

'D'you think you'll find your crack in the cliffs all right, Derek?' Lovat asked his second-in-command.

'Yes, there's no need to worry,' the latter replied with a conviction he was far from feeling.

By 0430 hours Mills-Roberts's group was approaching the beach. Sur-prisingly enough the lighthouse was flashing, its beam sweeping across the

H.Q. LT. COL. LORD

B'TROOP

BLANCMENIL
LE BAS WOOD

'F' TROOP

M.G.

BATTERY

MORTAR O.P.
FORCE BATTLE
H.Q.

SECTN
'A' TP

'C' TROOP

'C' TROOP

VASTERIVAL

POINTE D'AIL

MILLS ROBERTS
TION OF 'A' TROOP
ND 'C' TROOP

Assault by No 4 Commando on the
six gun battery West of Dieppe

MAIN ASSAULT

E W

N

Ste MARGUERITE

MAIN ASSAULT

R.

EAST END OF CLIFFS

EASTEN

LT.COL. LORD L
1 SECTN OF 'A'
'B' TROOP, 'F' T
H.Q.

=== A.A. GUNS   TELEPHONE
                       WIRE
=== HEAVY GUNS
                       XXXXXXX   BARBED
     STRONG   WIRE
     POINTS

landing-craft. 'We felt like thieves in an alley when the policeman's torch shines,' Mills-Roberts wrote later.

The craft were within a mile of the lighthouse when it suddenly doused. Tracer rose into the sky as Brewster Buffaloes roared inland at cliff-top level. It seemed that surprise must have been lost and the landing craft moved in at their best speed. Close to the cliff they turned to port, cruising along until Lieutenant David Style, sharper eyed than his seniors, spotted the landing place.

Running in the men had a dry landing – it was high tide – and in a matter of seconds were close under the cliff. Style's section reconnoitred the gullies. The left one was choked with thick wire and falls of chalk. A patrol on the flank passed a message: 'There's someone on top of the cliff'. Anxious moments followed as the wire in the right-hand gully was blown with Bangalore torpedoes, but still there was no interference. Fortunately the explosions coincided with heavy firing farther down the coast.

It took some time to reach the top of the promontory between the two gullies, but at length Mills-Roberts and his men were moving towards the villas of the little seaside resort of Vasterival-sur-Mer. He noticed that the gardens looked wild and unkempt. Style's section were searching the houses, and soon produced an old gentleman in a night-shirt, whose garden they had invaded. He seemed very surprised when told that the soldiers were not German but British. The major saw a pretty girl watching from the verandah.

'Are you going to shoot Papa?' she enquired philosophically.

It was now about 0540 hours and, despite delays in the gully, things were going according to plan, for the group still had twenty-five minutes before it had to be in position.

Suddenly, with a tremendous crash, the battery opened fire, and almost immediately the Intelligence Officer, Tony Smith, sent a wireless message from the beach. 'Convoy in sight, apparently within range of enemy battery.' The convoy appeared to be well ahead of schedule. Mills-Roberts decided to dispense with searching the houses between the beach and the

battery and to press on with speed.

'Corporal Smith and I, Ennis t Mortar Officer and our respecti signallers raced up through the woo I had just sent a message to Dav Style to join us at once. We hea the battery fire six salvoes in clo succession. The noise was deafenin It was heavy going, as the unde growth was waist high. We hear shooting on our right. Any idea pushing through 'the undergrow with stealth was out and we we crashing ahead like a herd of el phants.

'Suddenly the wood ended. W topped a little rise and came face t face with the battery itself. Ennis an I dropped; so did the others. We worke our way forward to a patch of scru some fifty yards in front of the woo and about a hundred yards from th perimeter wire of the battery. The was a good view from here and w heard the words of command di tinctly as the battery fired anothe salvo'.

Seeing a barn on the edge of th wood to his right Mills-Robert crawled back to the wood and ra there to find that he now had 'a magn ficent view of the six big guns and th crews serving them' only about 17 yards away. He was just in time t see the three right-hand guns fire salvo. A sniper settled himself on table and took careful aim.

'At last the rifle cracked, it was bull's-eye and one of the Master Rac took a toss into the gun pit. His com rades looked shocked and surprised I could see it all through my glasses It seemed rather like shooting men bers of a church congregation fro the organ loft'.

The major could not help wonder ing 'how prompt and how effective th German retaliation would be'. Davi Style's section dispersed in the bar area had begun to snipe the gun pit with rifle and Bren gun. The Germans first reaction was to take cover.

'The gun pits had small parapet of sandbags and the crews kept lov within them; and we could now se no movement between the variou battery buildings. Over on the righ there was movement, and the thre right-hand guns fired: no doubt the had been loaded before we had started in and whatever happened they must not be given the chance to load again. We expected trouble, but we did not relish the idea of having those large six-inch guns turned on us. It was up to us to see that they did not load again, either to shell the main convoy or to attempt to destroy the smaller fry to their immediate front'.

The Germans opened up with a 20mm gun from a high flak tower on stilts. The weapon had an all-round traverse. It began to rake the edge of the wood with a stream of phosphorescent shells, which burst against the tree trunks. Fortunately the gunners tended to fire high. A heavy machine-gun, probably the one at the north-east corner of the battery, put a wild burst into the wood.

'Suddenly over from some farm buildings on the extreme left of the battery came the phut, phut, phut of German mortars and soon all round us resounded the crash of mortar fire.'

The wood was becoming decidely unhealthy and Style moved half his section into the scrub, so that they could deal with the eastern end of the battery, as well as being less of a concentrated target.

By this time Mills-Roberts had been joined by two men, Gunner McDonough and Private Davis, with a Boys anti-tank rifle, a long and ponderous weapon, which was already obsolete. But if it would no longer pierce the tanks of the day it proved most effective against the flak tower, which suddenly ceased to revolve.

McDonough could now turn his attentions to the seven heavy machine-guns, sited in the perimeter wire. These had been located beforehand from the air photographs, and were already under accurate fire from the three Bren guns. But the German mortars, as yet unmolested, were still making things uncomfortable, especially in the barn area, where a 2-inch mortar detachment now came into action. Its first bomb fell short; 'but their next round was a good one and landed in a stack of cordite, behind Number 1 gun, which ignited with a stupendous crash, followed by shouts and yells of pain. We could see the Germans as they rushed forward with buckets and fire extinguishers,

and everything we had was directed on to this area. The fire grew, and meanwhile the big guns remained silent.'

It was 0607 hours.

The Germans were still fighting back. Mills-Roberts had a narrow escape when a mortar bomb landed in a tree above his head, and brought a heavy branch down beside him. Several men had been hit and the medical sergeant, Garthwaite, was mortally wounded, as he went to the assistance of Private Knowles. Another man, Fletcher, 'had all his equipment, and half his clothes blown off by a mortar bomb, while he himself was unhurt'. Style moved his men out of the garden and deployed them further to his left. McDonough and Davis, however, maintained their position in the living quarter of the barn, and when the flak tower opened up again returned its fire with good effect. As the German mortar fire grew still heavier Mills-Roberts's position became ever more precarious. But now, at long last, his 3-inch mortar detachment came into action, and wireless touch was made with Lovat's group. At 0625 hours the battery area was deluged with 2-inch mortar smoke and three minutes later the cannon fighters roared in for their two-minute strike at the guns. On the far side of the battery a Very light soared into the sky. It was the signal for the assault.

Lovat's group, five landing craft (LCAs) and one support craft (LCS), had also increased speed, when at 0430 hours they had seen the white star shells going up from the lighthouse.

Disembarking in the half light they came under fire from mortars and machine-guns as they crossed the heavy beach wire. There were twelve casualties. The Germans were firing tracer, which to men who had not been under fire before seemed most unpleasant. But in fact the casualties were mostly caused by the mortar, which, fortunately, lifted and tried to engage the landing craft as they withdrew.

Three Boston light bombers passed overhead, drawing the enemy fire as the Commandos crossed the wire and dashed across the Quiberville St Mar-

Above: Making smoke to cover the supporting vessels. *Below:* the reception

Above: A Boston over the lodgment area. *Right:* 4 Commando return to Newhaven. Captain Gordon Webb – with arm in sling

guerite road to gain the cover of the east bank of the River Saane. A stream of tracer bullets was whizzing past at about head height. Donald Gilchrist, a subaltern in the leading troop (B) wrote: 'We were forced to run like half-shut knives, our bodies bent forward, as if we were forcing our way against a strong wind.' Lieutenant Veasey scaled the cliff at the east end of the beach, using tubular ladders, and stormed the two pillboxes, sited to defend it. One proved to be unoccupied: the occupants of the other were killed with grenades.

The going was heavy in the long grass for the river had flooded its banks, but by 0515 hours the group had reached the bend where it must break from the cover of the bank and begin its dash eastwards. By this time it was broad daylight. In the distance sustained firing could be heard as Mills-Roberts's group engaged the battery.

The ground between the river and the little wood where the assault force was to form up was not entirely devoid of cover, and open patches were crossed in loose formation by bounds. Reaching the wood B Troop (Webb) and F Troop (Pettiward) divided, according to plan, and began working their way forward towards their forming-up areas.

Through a thick hedge men of B Troop spotted the flak tower. 'Gordon Webb gave the order to fire,' Gilchrist recalls. 'Rifles cracked. We watched amazed as a German soldier toppled over the edge and slowly fell to the ground some eighty feet below – like an Indian from a cliff in a western picture'. Webb sent Gilchrist and a small party to knock out the right hand gun.

'We cut across a hedge, raced through some trees, and darted between two buildings. Before us, not seventy-five yards away, was the battery position, German heads bobbing up and down. We began to stalk – we'd learned how to at Achnacarry – walking upright, stiff-legged, our weapons at the ready. Suddenly we froze.

A German soldier had appeared from a hedge which ran parallel to and behind the battery. He was carrying a box of grenades.'

Instead of surrendering the man began to shout 'Kommando, Kommando!' like one demented, whereon one of Gilchrist's men, remarking 'I'll give him f— Commando!' shot him. Trooper Marshall got another with his Bren, and someone else landed a hand-grenade in a machine-gun nest. 'Every time a coconut,' said a Cockney voice.

B Troop came under inaccurate fire as it moved round the southern edge of the wood and using the tactics of fire and movement with covering smoke, infiltrated through the orchard to its assembly position, just short of the battery buildings.

At 0625 hours Webb reported by wireless that he was in position for the final assault.

F Troop went through the wood to the point where the track running north leaves it. Thence they advanced under cover of smoke. Reaching a farmyard their scouts came upon a platoon of infantry clustered round the rear of a truck. Firing from the hip, with Bren and Tommy guns, Commandos came round the corner and wiped them out. Thus they disposed of the local 'riot squad' just as it was forming up and drawing grenades and ammunition as a preliminary, no doubt, to a counterattack against Mills-Roberts.

From here on F Troop met with stiff opposition from Germans ensconced in the buildings and enclosures just inside the perimeter of the battery. Pettiward was killed at the head of his men, struck by a stick grenade, and Lieutenant Macdonald was mortally wounded. A sergeant took their place, but was himself killed. Lovat's small HQ group included Captain Pat Porteous, whose role was to ensure liaison between the two assault groups. Porteous now ran across to F Troop, and, taking command, prepared to lead them to the charge. A German attacked him and shot him in the wrist, but Porteous managed to dispose of this assailant with his other hand.

At 0630 hours as the Spitfires of 129 Squadron made off, their brief strike completed, Lovat fired a series of white Very lights, and the assault went in. Webb, whose right wrist had been broken by a mortar bomb on the beach, led his yelling men firing his revolver with his left hand.

'Screams, smoke, the smell of burning cordite. Mad moments soon over'. Thus Gilchrist describes F Troop's part in taking the Varengeville Battery. One ugly episode remained in his mind. He and his men heard a shot and saw a German emerge from a barn and crash his boots into the face of a wounded Commando soldier. A corporal shot the man in the pit of the stomach.

'We doubled across the yard to where the two wounded lay side by side. For our comrade – morphine. For the beast – a bayonet thrust.'

While B Troop cleared the battery buildings Porteous led F Troop with dauntless courage to take the gun sites. Shot through the thigh he was still the first man into the guns, leading the men in a desperate bayonet charge which carried each gun-pit in turn. Troop Sergeant-Major Portman backed him up nobly. Mills-Roberts records that Porteous and Portman 'killed all of one German gun crew and then charged the next gun pit and seized it.'

When a grenade removed the whole of one heel Portman sat on the ground cooly picking off Germans with his rifle. Such was the spirit of the men Lovat led that day. They were not exactly in the mood to be repulsed.

The Germans fought with creditable obstinacy, defending themselves in underground tunnels, the cookhouse and other buildings. Their commanding officer is said to have been bayonetted after an exhilarating chase round the battery office. When the fighting fit ebbed away there were dead Germans everywhere, some badly burnt by cordite. There were only four prisoners, for isolated resistance from mutually supporting pillboxes continued even after the assault had carried the actual gun positions.

The work of demolition began.

Jimmy MacKay (B Troop) told Gilchrist in a satisfied tone that his

Captain Pat Porteous VC

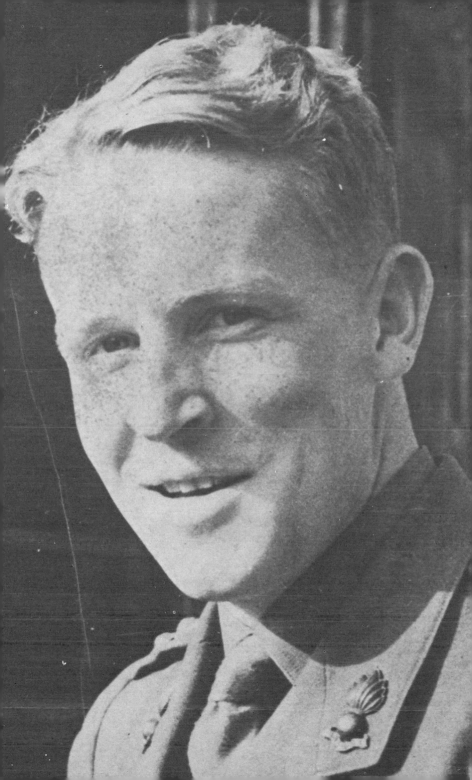

made-up charges had fitted the guns just like a glove'.

The same officer heard Lovat, a debonair figure 'in corduroy slacks and a grey sweater' and armed with a Winchester sporting rifle, give the order 'Set them on fire! Burn the lot,' indicating with a gesture the battery buildings, and comments 'They were the words of a Highland chief bent on the total destruction of the enemy'. It was not only Fraser of Lovat that was motivated by atavistic urges that day. To the British soldier of 1942 Dunkirk was very recent history, and he was tired of hearing about German supermen.

With the Varengeville Battery utterly demolished 4 Commando withdrew in good order, falling back through Robert Dawson's troop, which formed the perimeter round the beach where Mills-Roberts had landed.

It would be hard to conceive of a better planned *coup de main*, or one carried through with more determination. It cost 4 Commando forty-five casualties, including two officers and ten other ranks killed and four missing. Of the twenty wounded, twelve were back at duty within two months. Several of them, like Captain Webb and Lieutenant Style, had carried on after they were hit. The Germans lost not less than 150 killed.

The secrets of this stirring affair were meticulous planning, training and briefing, relentless yet imaginative leadership, and first-class weapon training, the foundation of that self-confidence which is the backbone of courage. In this exploit many won decorations, including the Victoria Cross which was awarded to Captain Pat Porteous.

The task of silencing the Berneval Battery fell to the lot of 3 Commando, the unit which eight months earlier had destroyed the German garrison of Vaagso. Durnford-Slater, who was still in command, decided upon a plan very similar in outline to Lovat's. A strong group under his own command was to land at the beach known as Yellow 1, and a smaller group under the second-in-command, Major Young, was to land at Yellow 2. The plan,

broadly speaking, was to assemble in rear of the battery, near Berneval Church, and to assault the battery in three waves, assault, support and reserve. It was felt that the battery, with perhaps 200 men, would succumb to such an attack by some 450 picked infantrymen. The unit's task was made more difficult because an assault ship was not available and it had to make the whole voyage from Newhaven in 'Eurekas'. These were wooden landing craft, lacking even the thin armour of the LCA. Each craft could carry eighteen fully equipped soldiers.

Number 3 Commando had not been less meticulous in its training than Number 4, but on this occasion Durnford-Slater's usual good fortune deserted him.

At 0347 hours the flotilla ran into a German convoy which was on passage from Boulogne to Dieppe and in the subsequent gun battle was scattered. The SGB in which the colonel had taken passage was hard hit, with forty per cent of its crew and passengers killed or wounded, and in a very short time was out of action. The destroyers which should have escorted the twenty landing craft had gone off up channel for some reason best known to their senior officer, the commander of the Polish warship *Slazak*, and were thus denied the pleasure of an action with five German vessels, which would probably have been easy meat to them.

A number of the Eurekas were more of less severely damaged, whilst others had broken down even before the sea fight began; they were not designed for a seventy mile channel crossing.

It is not possible for me to discuss this operation in the dispassionate terms of a military commentator since, as it chances, I was second-in-command of Number 3 Commando in this action. I trust I will be forgiven, therefore, if an element of personal reminiscence creeps into the military history at this point!

In the first place I may say that the whole operation seemed 'pretty dicey'. I recall vividly that as we sailed from Newhaven in the dusk I consoled myself with the thought that having survived Dunkirk, Guernsey, Lofoten

145

Above: A German medical orderly treats a wounded Canadian. *Below:* A field dressing station. *Right:* 4 Commando disembark at Newhaven

and Vaagso, I had had a fair run for my money.

The sea-fight was a very unpleasant experience. With streams of tracer converging on the wooden landing craft it seemed that death was but an instant away. When the SGB reeled out of action we turned to starboard and made our escape, but in doing so lost contact with all the other landing craft.

Unworthy thoughts assailed me. What good could one do with only eighteen men? However, the officer in charge of our craft, Lieutenant-Commander Buckee, was as skilful as resolute. After a time he said:

'There you are, there's your beach'.

'What do we do now,' I asked, rather pointlessly.

'My orders', he replied, 'are to land even if there's only one boat'.

This aroused the innate obstinacy, or 'bloody-mindedness' which I recognize as one of the less charming facets of my character.

'Those are my orders, too,' I replied. 'We are to land whatever happens, even if we have to swim'.

There are those who contend that the Dieppe raid was not a surprise. To this I can only reply that we could see a lighthouse flashing as we ran in, and that the trenches of the platoon position where we landed were unoccupied. We hit the beach at 0450 hours – five minutes early – and some twenty minutes later had managed to climb the cliff, hauling ourselves up by the barbed wire. The Germans are thorough people and they had put it the whole way up the cliff. The pegs made good footholds. It was daylight when we reached the top and we could see five other landing craft running in to Yellow 1. We could also see the back of a notice board. Walking round to the inland side we read the words ACHTUNG MINEN, but by that time we were through the minefield. I assembled my eighteen followers in a small copse, and gave them the benefit of my views on minor tactics, as well as some rather unconvincing exhort-ations of the 'Once more unto the breach' variety. Then we set off, moving with a caution that proved unwarran-ted. The first civilian we met assured

us that there were 200 Germans in the battery.

Before we reached the village the battery opened fire, and throwing caution to the winds we ran down the street to the church, where we hoped to meet the men who had landed from Yellow 1. Instead we came under fire from a German machine-gun, which luckily fired high, bringing a shower of tiles about our ears.

I hoped to snipe the German gunners from the church tower, but the sexton had removed the ladder. Then we tried to work our way up through the orchard behind the battery, but we kept getting fired at by unseen rifle-men, and this seemed unpromising. I assembled the party at the western edge of the orchard, where I could see a great cornfield that lay between our landing place and the battery. I decided to deploy the party on the flank of the battery and snipe at the gunners. Some of my followers did not seem altogether persuaded of the beauty of this scheme, but I explained to them that it was well known that nine feet of corn will stop a rifle bullet just as well as, say, eighteen inches of brickwork will.

We doubled out into the field and re-deployed in two lines with big intervals between each man so that the second line could fire through the first. This worked rather well. We had one Bren, but most of the men were armed with rifles. We kept up a steady but not rapid fire, as I wanted to conserve ammunition.

Though we were not 200 yards from the battery our view was not particu-larly good, as the guns were on the same level as ourselves. We had to fire from the kneeling position, crawling to fresh positions after one or two rounds, and I cannot claim that we caused many casualties for the gun-ners had low concrete walls to hide behind. Still, if we missed Number 4 Gun, Number 2 would have the benefit of the crack and thump as our bullets winged their way by.

I suppose the gunners fired fifteen or twenty rounds out to sea. I do not think they fired any salvoes. Eventu-ally they got bored with us. Suddenly there was a great explosion, almost in our faces it seemed, though it must have been 150 yards away, an orange

Light naval craft cover the withdrawal

flash and a cloud of black smoke. A shell wandered over our heads and landed behind us somewhere in France. The Germans had swung the left hand gun round and were having a go at us. Luckily they could not depress sufficiently to do any harm. Even so it was rather a shattering moment, and the soldier next to me said indignantly: 'Sir! We're being mortared!' Not a very accurate description of the fire of a 6-inch gun.

At Varengeville the Germans had used their mortars to some effect. They do not seem to have had any at Berneval.

Highland chief returns from raid

They fired their gun at us four times, and we greeted each shot with a volley. Then they gave it up as a bad job. Perhaps they saw that they were not hitting us. Perhaps we knocked out the crew. Weighing the situation impersonally it was, of course, much better that they should fire at us than at the shipping off Dieppe. Looking that way all one could see was a great bank of smoke. From Berneval it was not possible to identify a single target off the town.

Ammunition began to run low and it was clearly only a matter of time until the Germans would produce some force, perhaps supported by tanks, to put in a counterattack.

After shooting up the observation post on the cliff, we withdrew. We had had two casualties, but both got away. Buckee had kept his landing craft close into the shore, and we got aboard in the nick of time. Major Blücher and some assault engineers of 181 Division followed us up, and a section reached the cliff in time to fire at us as we departed. In the exchange that followed one of the sailors was hit in the thigh, and a German rifle fell down the cliff.

The craft that landed at Yellow 1 comprised men of several troops. Two of the craft belonged to my old 6 Troop, under Captain Dick Wills, the senior officer present. He led them through a deep bank of wire and thrust inland with vigour. Corporal Banger Halls took a machine gun post, charging single-handed with the bayonet, and a determined effort was made to fan out from the narrow gully. Rhodes, Will's runner, was shot in the forearm, had himself patched up, and rejoined his officer with one hand looped round his neck by a bandage and the other grasping an automatic.

The Germans had seen the craft run in, and evidently launched their reserve platoon to hem them in. This left them nothing to spare to counterattack my party, which, having landed in the dark, was presumably undetected until it reached the church.

Advancing up a narrow road, bordered by villas and hedges, the group made slow progress. Wills, whose eyesight was not remarkable, accounted for one German – probably the best shot of his life – but soon afterwards was shot through the neck. With his fall the momentum went out of the attack, and eventually German reinforcements arrived in considerable force, and the survivors were compelled to surrender.

Despite the ill-fortune that attended Number 3 Commando the Berneval Battery does not appear to have

After Dieppe: the raiding phase closes

scored any hits on the numerous vessels that lay off Dieppe during the raid. It would ill befit me to claim any special significance for this action, but I owe it to the men who were with me that day to say that they played their part with all the *sang froid* which down the years has been the hall-mark of the British soldier at his best.

The Dieppe raid was a costly affair. The Royal Navy had 550 casualties, and lost a destroyer as well as a number of landing craft. Military casualties, mostly Canadian, numbered 3,670 and material lost included twenty-nine Churchill tanks. The Germans admitted a loss of 591 men as well as a number of guns. The Royal Air

Force lost 153 officers and men and 106 planes. The Germans admitted the loss of forty-eight aircraft. Except for 4 Commando's brilliant feat, it cannot be said that the operation was a great success. But it showed the planners that the Allies were not likely to take a port in France on D-Day, whenever that day should dawn. In consequence it was decided to land over the open beaches, towing the Mulberry Harbour, that famous pre-fabricated port, all the way to France. Thus, as so often in war, the right thing happened for the wrong reason.

The soldier's life is full of ups and downs, and the man that cannot take that had better remain a civilian. So I will conclude this sad chapter with a merry tale. It seems that the Germans were very excited at capturing their first Americans, some Rangers who were attached to the Commandos. One, a man of immense height, whose name I wish I could transmit to history, was being interrogated.

German Officer: 'How many American soldiers are there in England?'

US Ranger: 'There are three million. They are all as tall as I am and they have to be kept behind barbed wire to stop them swimming the Channel to get at you bastards.'

Fortunately this particular German had a sense of humour.

Epilogue

'One man is no more than another, if he do no more than what another does.'

The Commando story did not end in 1942, but with the invasion of North Africa on 7th November the whole nature of their role changed. Now began the great series of Allied counter-offensives whose relentless pressure brought the war to an end, with Hitler dead in the ruins of Berlin. In this period of the war, which lasted for approximately two and a half years, the main role of the Commandos was to spearhead large-scale landings by conventional forces, rather than to carry out raids, al-though sometimes, notably ·on the east coast of the Adriatic, their mission remained that of those first two years when they had set themselves to torment the *Wehrmacht* between Narvik and Bayonne.

Hard fighting lay ahead for those Commando units that still survived in 1942. Number 1, after a long and hard campaign in North Africa, was to distinguish itself in Burma, during the last campaign on the Arakan

coast, especially in the decisive battle of Kangaw. Number 2, rebuilt by Lieutenant-Colonel Jack Churchill after St Nazaire, won further laurels at Salerno and on the shores of the Adriatic. Number 3, after two landings in Sicily and the battle of Termoli, took part in the D-Day landings, went through the whole of the campaign in Normandy, and, later, fought with the Second Army in its advance from the Maas to the Baltic. It may be asserted that no Commando saw more active service than Number 3, though but few of the men that captured Vaagso were still with the unit by the time it crossed the Aller.

Number 4 Commando was another that took part in the long advance from Normandy to the Baltic. At Ouistreham on D-Day, and on Walcheren, it was to display once more the verve and dash of the days when Lord Lovat led it into the Varengeville Battery at Dieppe.

Number 5 Commando, after taking part in the conquest of Madagascar, went to the Arakan, where it played a decisive part in the battle of Kangaw. Number 6 shared with Number 1 the dangers and discomforts of the Tunisian campaign, proving a match for the Hermann Göring Jäger. Later it was with the 1st Commando Brigade in Normandy, Holland and Germany. A unit remarkable for its disciplined courage and its professional skill, it had a moment of sheer, old-fashioned panache, when, with hunting horns sounding and bayonets fixed, it cleared the Aller woods on 8th April, 1945.

Most of Number 9 Commando's active service was in Italy, and the most memorable of its battles was probably the crossing of Lake Comachio.

The various troops of Number 10 (Inter-Allied) Commando, formed under Lieutenant-Colonel Dudley Lister in January 1942, shared the adventures of the British Commandos. The Belgians and Poles, for example, were with Number 2 at Salerno, while the French were with Number 4 in France, and particularly distinguished themselves at the storming of Ouistreham.

Decorations, or the lack of them, are far from being a certain guide to the military virtue of an individual. Many a dogged and skilful soldier has gone through much hard fighting without any special recognition beyond campaign stars, which, after all, are awarded to everyone present who is not discharged with ignominy! Nevertheless the number of awards for gallantry is a useful indication of the effectiveness of a unit or formation. Commando soldiers were awarded eight Victoria Crosses, thirty-seven DSOs and in addition nine bars to that award, 162 Military Crosses with thirteen bars, thirty-two Distinguished Conduct Medals, and 218 Military Medals. In an army where honours and awards were not distributed in lavish fashion, this total of 479 speaks for itself.

Although the Victoria Cross is the only British decoration which can be awarded posthumously a number of the Commando soldiers who won awards did not survive the war. Five officers took part in the raid on Sark. They were Major Geoffrey Appleyard, Captains Colin Ogden-Smith, Dudgeon and Philip Pinkney, and the Dane,

Lieutenant Andy Lassen. Between them they won a VC, a DSO, and six MCs, but unhappily not one of the five lived to see the end of the war. These were exceptionally severe casualties, but other Commandos paid for their triumphs with their persons. When Number 3 Commando went to Normandy in 1944 there were only two officers and a score of men who had been with the unit when it formed. Vaagso, Agnone, and Termoli had taken their toll.

The First Commando Brigade went to Normandy with four units, Numbers 3, 4, 6 and 45 (Royal Marine) Commandos. The Brigadier, Lord Lovat, was badly wounded by a shell during the attack on Breville. Lieutenant-Colonel Robert Dawson (4 Commando) was badly wounded in the assault on Ouistreham, as was the commander of his French troops, Commandant Philippe Kieffer. Derek Mills-Roberts (6 Commando) received a nasty wound in the leg during the defence of Le Plein, but, with his customary resolution, remained to command the Brigade; his second-in-command, Bill Coade, had been hit in the face by a stick grenade on D-Day. On D-Day the commander of Number 3 Commando was twice hit by fragments of shell, while the second-in-command, Major John Pooley, MC, who had been in all the unit's exploits since June 1940, fell in the Merville Battery. The CO of 45 (RM), Charles Ries, was twice wounded on D-Day, and of the brigade's hierarchy only one CO and Major Nicol Grey survived the campaign undamaged.

Not all the Commandos were as unfortunate in this respect as the officers of the Special Boat Section. Of those whose fortunes we have followed in these pages a number went on to play their part in the later phases of the war when the Allies were on the offensive. Charles Haydon and Bob Laycock became major-generals, and the latter was to succeed Lord Mountbatten as Chief of Combined Operations. Lord Lovat, Derek Mills-Roberts, and Peter Young successively commanded the First Commando Brigade, while at the end of the war Ronnie Tod was commanding the Second, and John Durnford-Slater had

risen to be Deputy Commander of Commando Group. Newman, taken at St Nazaire, was to spend the rest of the war 'in the bag', but was treated with respect by his captors, who even held a parade to celebrate the announcement of the award to him of the Victoria Cross. His successor, the fiery Jack Churchill, after countless adventures, was captured in Yugoslavia. He proved an elusive prisoner and, after several daring attempts, managed to escape during the chaotic final weeks of the war.

A few of the regular soldiers continued in the army after the war, serving in Korea, Jordan and elsewhere. As late as 1969 Brigadier Denis O'Flaherty and Colonel Pat Porteous were still serving. By that date time was beginning to take its toll of the men who a generation earlier had volunteered for special service. There

are many who take pleasure in imagining that 'Britain is finished', and one would have to be complacent indeed to see the England of 1969 as some sort of Utopia. But there was little for comfort in our situation in 1940, and there were plenty of ancient warriors willing to proclaim that the country no longer bred men like the soldiers of the Somme and Passchendaele. No doubt the veterans of Agincourt and Edgehill, of Blenheim and Waterloo, had sung the same song. Nothing is more boring to a young man than to be told that 'things are not what they were'. The Commando soldiers of 1940 may have been rather special in their way – they were all picked volunteers. But they were far from regarding themselves as anything out of the ordinary. Few were of gigantic stature, and, until they had received their specialist

158

training, few were exceptionally skilful in the martial arts. The great majority had never even been under fire. They were just fed up with being told the Germans were supermen and that they themselves were 'wet'. And so they revolted against their age and went to war in a new spirit of dedicated ferocity. They rejected the lotus years. The politicians of the League of Nations, of Disarmament and of Munich had lost their allegiance, if they ever had it. They revelled in the luxury of responding to uncompromising leadership in a cause that needed no explanation. They approached new tasks in a critical spirit. No tactic was sound just because the book said so. The men who rammed the lock-gates at St Nazaire did a deed every bit as daring as the charge of the Light Brigade at Balaclava, but the old

attitude of 'their's not to reason why' was gone.

A Commando leader once jested bitterly, saying 'An officer is always wrong until he's proved right'. The Commando soldier expected, and rightly, to be clearly briefed; to 'know what he was on'. This was the secret of success in a hundred fights. Intelligent men knew the object of the operation; if things went wrong, if leaders fell, they could use their training, and their native wit, to improvise and to carry on. Battle tactics are no longer the 'Load! Present! Fire!' business of Wellington's day. Happy the commander who has keen, literate, motivated men to carry out his plans! And that is exactly what we had in the Commandos long ago.

Bibliography

Geoffrey J E Appleyard (Blandford Press, London)
Seven Assignments Brigadier Dudley Clarke (Jonathan Cape, London)
The Vaagso Raid Major Joseph H Devins Jr (Robert Hale, London)
Commando Brigadier J F Dunford-Slater (William Kimber, London)
The Watery Maze Bernard Fergusson (Collins, London)
Castle Commando Donald Gilchrist (Oliver and Boyd, London)
Combined Operations 1940–1942 (HMSO, London)
Commando Attack Gordon Holman (Hodder and Stoughton, London)
Geoffrey Keyes of the Rommel Raid Elizabeth Keyes (George Newnes Ltd, Londc
Tobruk Commando Gordon Landsborough (Cassell, London)
The Fillbusters John Lodwick (Methuen, London)
The Greatest Raid of All CE Lucas Phillips (Heinemann, London)
Clash by Night Brigadier D Mills-Roberts (William Kimber, London)
The Attack on St Nazaire Commander RED Ryder VC (John Murray, London)
The Green Beret Hilary St. George Saunders (Michael Joseph, London)
Storm from the Sea Brigadier P Young (William Kimber, London)